"Dr. MelindaJoy Mingo brings a fresh, new, and powerful voice in the arena of unity, diversity, and the role of the gospel in moving us beyond past hurts to the beauty and joy of cultivating and sustaining diverse relationships. The winsome art of personal storytelling from around the world allows us to follow the message of the value and worth of all people while pointing to deeper implications of change that occur when we allow the truth of the gospel to bring transformation in our lives. This book presents a timely and compelling message not just for this generation but for generations to come."

John M. Perkins, cofounder and president emeritus of the John and Vera Mae Perkins Foundation and Christian Community Development Association

"The thoughts in this book are critical and vital. With its practical suggestions, reading *The Colors of Culture* will help you strike up a conversation with your peers to grow, impact your city, and transform the next generation."

Gabriel Valle, founding pastor of Iglesia Venga Tu Reino and Colorado Springs coordinator for the National Day of Prayer Task Force

"Dr. Mingo has, for decades, lived out her counsel to be patient in forming friendships with those who are different than ourselves. She engages in courageous conversations in order to clear up misperceptions. I particularly appreciate her insights into how local churches can perhaps unthinkingly assign permanent visitor status to those who regularly attend but who come from a culture different from the majority."

Robert Rasmussen, executive director of Near Frontiers

"MelindaJoy encourages us to not get stuck in fear and be willing to initiate small steps toward befriending someone. It was those small steps MelindaJoy took that created the friendship we have treasured over the last fifteen years. The book also reminds us to pause, rethink, and reflect on our life's journey and consider how we are connecting with others."

Nga Pham, senior research officer, Australian Centre for Financial Studies, Monash Business School

"MelindaJoy Mingo is quite simply one of the finest leaders I have ever known. If you read this book, you will be inspired, but if you do what this book is asking, you will be forever changed. In *The Colors of Culture*, MelindaJoy Mingo teaches us how to think critically about inequality and diversity without getting mired in guilt or despair. Through her stories, she carefully explains why there's a social polarization within Christian communities of faith. Then with challenging directives, she shows us tangible ways this Christian culture of polarization can be repaired and even eradicated—when each of us pours love and compassion into being all that Christ calls us to be. This is one powerhouse book!"

H. Malcolm Newton, president of the Denver Institute of Urban Studies

"*The Colors of Culture* provides t cultural and racial understanding. While discussing diversity, Melin authen-ticity, transparency, and global e ols for us. Her terms such as *racial rigi* are so refreshing and biblical. MelindaJ isdom, and sensitivity. This book will be s."

Clarence Shuler (a.k.a. "The Love hips

"MelindaJoy Mingo has traveled the world, and *The Colors of Culture* gives us a glimpse into her journey. MelindaJoy provides a well-rounded, authentic perspective for engaging individuals from diverse cultures and backgrounds, including building relationships of mutual respect. Her approach of treating everyone with value, dignity, and worth truly embodies how she lives her life. *The Colors of Culture* is a must-read!"

Tiko Hardy, director of diversity and global learning at Pikes Peak Community College

"MelindaJoy Mingo not only talks the talk, she walks the walk. We have shared the stage at our church speaking about the very issues facing our culture today that she so beautifully handles in this book. The world needs more of Dr. Mingo. Every time I am around her I learn more. I cannot wait for you to experience her deep wisdom and passion, love, and compassion for all people as you read this much-needed message for our world today."

Greg Lindsey, lead pastor of Discovery Church Colorado

"A treatise on the love of neighbor, *The Colors of Culture* challenges us to move beyond the us-versus-them mentality, inviting us to see cultural differences through the eyes of Jesus. M. J. provides a comfortable and enjoyable read on the difficult subject of race and culture, uncovering her own personal biases and aha moments along the way. Her *Ubuntu* stories are transparent, offering the right handles to the basket of this important topic. The recommended practices are tried and tested principles that I have personally witnessed M. J. living out. I dare you to reflect on these truths, move out of your comfort zone, embrace the beauty of diverse friendships, and experience the difference it will make in your city."

Yemi Mobolade, entrepreneur, pastor, and cofounder of COSILoveYou

"The message in this book comes straight from our Holy Great Spirit Creator. Dr. MelindaJoy's compelling accounts of humanness come through both her personal life's encounters and how she has observed others. *The Colors of Culture* is a sacred bundle of wisdom and truly an eloquent delivery of raw remedy. I will strongly suggest this book to my First Nations people. *Pilamaya*~in gratitude."

Cahuilla K. M. Red Elk, retired tribal attorney, founder and CEO of the Center on Human Rights and American Indian Law Advocacy

"Seize the time and become richer in your understanding of how to reach diverse people groups. MelindaJoy has traveled around the world so that we can just travel to our mailboxes or online to read this book and learn from this timely and profound message."

Promise Lee, pastor, professor, author, and international liaison for social justice

the
colors
of
culture

the beauty
of diverse
friendships

melindajoy mingo

An imprint of InterVarsity Press
Downers Grove, Illinois

InterVarsity Press
P.O. Box 1400, Downers Grove, IL 60515-1426
ivpress.com
email@ivpress.com

InterVarsity Press® is the book-publishing division of InterVarsity Christian Fellowship/USA®, a movement of students and faculty active on campus at hundreds of universities, colleges, and schools of nursing in the United States of America, and a member movement of the International Fellowship of Evangelical Students. For information about local and regional activities, visit intervarsity.org.

All Scripture quotations, unless otherwise indicated, are taken from The Holy Bible, New International Version®, NIV®. Copyright © 1973, 1978, 1984, 2011 by Biblica, Inc.™ Used by permission of Zondervan. All rights reserved worldwide. www.zondervan.com. The "NIV" and "New International Version" are trademarks registered in the United States Patent and Trademark Office by Biblica, Inc.™

While any stories in this book are true, some names and identifying information may have been changed to protect the privacy of individuals.

Cover design and image composite: David Fassett
Interior design: Daniel van Loon
Images: hand silhouette: © PASHA18 / iStock / Getty Images Plus
      textured paper: © xamtiw / iStock / Getty Images Plus

ISBN 978-0-8308-4526-2 (print)
ISBN 978-0-8308-8760-6 (digital)

Printed in the United States of America ♾

InterVarsity Press is committed to ecological stewardship and to the conservation of natural resources in all our operations. This book was printed using sustainably sourced paper.

Library of Congress Cataloging-in-Publication Data
A catalog record for this book is available from the Library of Congress.

P	21	20	19	18	17	16	15	14	13	12	11	10	9	8	7	6	5	4	3	2	1
Y	37	36	35	34	33	32	31	30	29	28	27	26	25	24	23	22	21	20			

contents

introduction

We are living during a time in our society when fear and mistrust among people of different racial groups are becoming the norm rather than the exception. Acknowledging that there has been a huge resurgence of racism, discrimination, and individual prejudices is difficult and even baffling at times. The cultural divide appears to be expanding rather than shrinking. Although we have made great strides in learning how to connect with people beyond our discomforts and fears and to see others as God sees them, as people of value and worth, if we are honest, there is still much work to be done.

Cultural mistrust does not only come from our obvious differences such as race or lifestyle—how we treat each other as individuals and our perception of each other both play a role as well. At a recent town hall meeting in my city to discuss what steps we can take to understand each other better, a young woman stated, "I thought we were past all this divisive *stuff*. I just think we have fear of each other and we have to learn how to trust and respect each other again."

It was an uncomfortable meeting, with raw conversations centered on the role of law enforcement in our city and the mistrust among communities of color due to both national and local events involving blacks and community policing. A courageous conversation took place in a room filled with people who barely knew each other but wanted to begin the necessary process to move beyond shallow words and mistrust to building bridges instead of walls.

That one meeting has initiated many more in our city, and friendships have formed between the most unlikely people. They would never have happened without people being willing to take steps to pursue understanding each other.

While we do have some heartbreaking problems happening daily in our society regarding interactions between diverse populations, it is my belief that we have solutions that will take courage to move beyond our places of comfort. But these solutions are not as complicated as we make them. What can we do? We can learn to see every human being from God's perspective as persons of worth, value their lived experiences even when we don't understand them, and cultivate genuine relationships based on humility, vulnerability, and transparency.

If we are not willing to get real about our own heart issues with people from different cultures and backgrounds, and if we don't allow God to bring healing, nothing will change in our lives or in the lives of those we interact with daily. Sometimes it's easier to ask Jesus to change the situations around us rather than transform ourselves and allow the change to begin within us.

Almost every African Bantu dialect includes the saying, "I am because we are," which is captured by the term *Ubuntu*. The word literally means "human-ness" and roughly translates to "human kindness." The concept of Ubuntu is that, no matter our differences, we as human beings can connect with one another through sharing our life experiences, stories, and humanity. We all have stories from our journeys in life, and our stories and lived experiences are the heart of who we are. And even though our life stories do not always connect with the stories of others, they are an important summation of our personal experiences, of why we believe as we do, and ultimately of our frame of reference and our perspective of others.

My first introduction to the term *Ubuntu* came through a fascinating picture of a group of people with linked arms running together to get a small basket of sweet treats—just enough treats for one person, really. A caption explained that the group had been told that the person who reached the basket first would get the treats. When they were asked why they ran together instead of individually, their response was, "Ubuntu—how can one of us be happy if the other ones are sad?" I was still puzzled about why they would run together when there was only one prize and why that would make

3

them genuinely happy. I also wondered what that all had to do with culture and relationships.

I finally got the message when I read the following words by Archbishop Desmond Tutu, which are a rich description of how we should ultimately connect with any person from any culture.

It is the essence of being human. It speaks of the fact that my humanity is caught up and is inextricably bound up in yours. I am human because I belong. It speaks about wholeness, it speaks about compassion. A person with Ubuntu is welcoming, hospitable, warm and generous, willing to share.

- *Such people are open and available to others, willing to be vulnerable, affirming of others, do not feel threatened that others are able and good, for they have a proper self-assurance that comes from knowing that they belong in a greater whole. They know that they are diminished when others are humiliated, diminished when others are oppressed, diminished when others are treated as if they were less than who they are. The quality of Ubuntu gives people resilience, enabling them to survive and emerge still human despite all efforts to dehumanize them.*

When genuine warmth, respect, and honor are displayed not merely for aesthetic purposes but out of genuine love and compassion for others—in other words, out of Ubuntu—a journey toward transparency, understanding, and long-lasting friendships is enabled.

From this, an idea evolved around my passion and love for seeing people from different cultures and backgrounds unite. I called it genuine Ubuntu relationships—the willingness to see every human being from God's perspective and not through the lens of prejudices, stereotypes, and negative societal influences. These Ubuntu relationships are not just about being warm and fuzzy with people from different cultures. They involve understanding that a common bond exists between us all as well as differences that we don't need to fear.

Our stories prove that although we are diverse in our perspectives and different from each other in very unique ways, our differences should not keep us from the things we have in common as followers of Christ and as human beings. We all experience joy and laughter, trials and triumphs, fear and trust, pain and disappointment. We ultimately become unified when we are willing to walk together, as uncomfortable as it might be, and not allow barriers such as race or class to make us forget that we really do have a lot more in common with each other than we believe.

Whether in our neighborhoods, churches, workplaces, or other spheres, community is built when we intentionally choose to come out of our comfort zones and connect to others without feeling like we are walking on eggshells. It means risking everything that we think we know about other cultures. It involves not getting stuck in fear and being willing to initiate small steps toward befriending someone.

It takes honesty to admit that even as followers of Jesus we can dislike people we know very little about because their values and beliefs are opposite to what we think or believe. But treating someone with dignity means seeing them as someone who deserves to be communicated with in a spirit of respect even if we don't agree with their lifestyle or beliefs. To truly connect with people who are different from us will take the grace of God.

When we are willing to learn what dignity, honor, and re-spect look like in different cultures, we not only positively affect diverse people and their communities, but we allow Jesus to work in our hearts as well. And through this bond of humanity and the pursuit of understanding each other we discover our own identity. We also gain a greater under-standing of what is written in the Bible about responding to those around us with love first. Jesus reminds us that the second greatest commandment is to love our neighbors as ourselves. And he will help us learn how to do that.

It is doubtful that any solitary person can reflect God's character on their own. God's image comes to expression in community and especially in our friendships with others. The journey of soul growth doesn't occur in isolation but rather through our relationships with others as our lives collide in our everyday dealings in a broken and hurting world. The truth is that relationships as a whole can be a bit messy, and learning how to truly relate to others takes time. But I believe most people are looking for genuine relationships and community. And relationships can be very beautiful and rewarding and reflect the heart of God for all humanity.

How to Use This Book

The first part of this book explores the connection between culture and identity, and helps bring clarity to ideas about history, cultural identity and bias, and humility. When you are open to building diverse friendships, you are also willing to go beyond surface layers to pursue true understanding with others. I hope this book will help you be more aware of some of these layers. This section includes a chapter about God's heart for diversity, grounding our relationships in Jesus and the Bible.

The second part of the book provides a way forward, giving practical steps for applying the concepts covered in part one and forging stronger diverse relationships. Throughout both sections are my own stories of the beauty of diverse friendships and how God has worked through them. My desire is that this book will be a guide for and bring encouragement to those who feel stuck but who desire to live out the beauty of God's diversity in their relationships. There are sections at the end of each chapter called a "Pause Moment," which offers questions that can be used for personal reflection or group interaction.

Because people often come to conversations about diversity with different definitions of words, I want to clarify a few before we start. I use the term *culture* to refer to specific and notable attributes of an individual or a group of people that distinguishes them from other groups. The term *worldview* refers to a network of ideas, feelings, and assumptions that gives a frame of reference to an individual or a group of people and shapes the reality of what they think, feel, or do. Finally, the words *ethnicity* and *ethnic groups* refer to a community or population composed of people who share a common cultural background or descent.

This book is a compilation of real stories and examples of people who embody the concept of Ubuntu relationships. The stories involve love, forgiveness, missed opportunities, and second chances. Some parts of the stories are messy. They reveal the reality that building relationships includes many obstacles and challenges, some of which are real and some of which are imagined due to our perceptions of different cultures. But I didn't want to write a book that would only highlight problems. I want to share real-life stories of what it looks like for Ubuntu relationships to be lived out even when the people involved didn't get it right the first time around. I wanted to show how relationship mistakes can become learning opportunities. For these reasons I have risked being transparent in sharing my stories—my successes and my failures. And I have received permission from others to share their stories.

However, for their privacy, names and identifying details have been changed.

The impact of historical racism, present-day cultural tensions, different life experiences, and differing personal values and beliefs in our twenty-first-century postmodern society have led to many misunderstandings among people of various cultures. But building relationships with others does not have to be complex if we choose to walk in humility, instead of posturing ourselves over any other culture, and simply enjoy the journey of doing life together. To do life together is to find commonalities that are shared with someone and from those commonalities begin to appreciate our differences.

Journeying Through This Book

As I wrote this book, I came face-to-face with old patterns of personal bias and prejudice. I also struggled with the desire to not offend.

I have had to take my own "pause moment" to reflect on what I have learned throughout life and what I continue to learn through a journey of personal racism and discrimination, rejection, and injustices. I have also had to earnestly look at my negative actions and behaviors toward, as well as words about, other cultures and not just what I have experienced.

Living out the fullness of the gospel means I have to stay true to what I believe about relationships with my friends from other cultures and not be persuaded by others' perspectives and experiences or anything that I see or hear in society today.

As you read the book, I have a request. Take a deep look within your soul at your current relationships with individuals from different cultures and assess if they truly model the example of Jesus. Ask God to rekindle a passion and joy in your heart as you develop skills for being a cultural champion—someone who learns how to bridge the gap between cultures, develops a greater level of comfort with diverse people groups, and helps others move from surface-only to authentic healthy relationships.

The best part of any book for me is the part that I can apply to my real-life circumstances. I am therefore writing about the real, courageous conversations that we are having behind closed doors—the conversations that address the questions, comments, and thoughts we would dare not utter in front of a stranger because we wouldn't want to look like we are prejudiced, racist, or even unspiritual.

At the root, this is a book of Ubuntu stories, and although race and class are talked about because it is a book about culture, it is ultimately about learning how to connect with anyone deeply at the heart level. It is about finding commonalities in our everyday life encounters with different people, and being aware of the God moments that occur in our relationships.

I have been privileged to travel around the world. I have traveled not only physically but also with my heart through beautiful villages in Vietnam, rugged roads in Kenya, jungles of the Dominican Republic, slums in Ethiopia, and communities in America where my "neighbors" come from different cultures. As I have traveled and built relationships with people different from me, I have learned—and continue to learn—that culture and diversity are not just a good idea but rather a God idea. He is the one who created us. We didn't decide our eye color, looks, language, or any other part of our cultural identity. God created everything about us on purpose, and when we view ourselves and others with the perspective that we are God's handiwork, we eliminate stereotypes. Each person has so much beauty, and every connection can leave deep handprints of love and respect for God's greatest masterpiece—his creation of us— regardless of our differences.

As you walk with me through these stories that mirror love, forgiveness, hope, and healing, I pray that you will also see your life as a beacon of hope for someone who just wants to have a friend who can appreciate who they genuinely are and who wants to be treated as a person of value, worth, and dignity.

PART ONE

the connection between culture and identity

history matters

Perhaps travel cannot prevent bigotry, but by demonstrating that all peoples cry, laugh, eat, worry, and die, it can introduce the idea that if we try and understand each other, we may even become friends.

MAYA ANGELOU

One day while drinking coffee, laughing, and sharing stories with one of my best friends, who is white, an unexpected question about race came up. It just popped up out of nowhere as we were talking about the possibility of taking a fun trip on a cruise together. My friend asked, "Why do we have a group called Black Lives Matter that is expanding so rapidly in our nation? I believe that it's a group that is being used to spread hate and division. We don't need a group like that."

Before I could answer, she went on to explain that she also now feels that because she is white, people from different racial groups who used to talk with her at her job are now ignoring her. With a trembling voice and tears, she said that everybody in life has seen injustices—not just a certain group of people. She also admitted to me that she is tired of seeing images on television of people marching and protesting, and that the playing field in America is now equal, so she doesn't understand why people can't just move on from the past. After all, she explained, none of the younger generation of white people in society today were a part of discrimination in the past. She said she was sorry about the pain that people have experienced but that she had nothing to do with placing signs on bathroom doors that read "colored" or "white." Her voice reached a place of pain that I had never heard as she proclaimed that she now feels like she is the victim of reverse discrimination in society. She ended her remarks by saying, "You know me. I am not a racist. I just have a lot of heart pain. I'm tired and confused."

My best friend is a committed believer and has one of the tenderest hearts toward people that I have ever seen. We have known each other for over twenty years, and I fondly refer to her as a blue-eyed soul queen, a name I gave her when I found out that she has spent years of living and building friendships within the black community. Whether it has been hanging out at traditional black soul food restaurants, swaying and clapping to the beat of gospel music, or just hanging with diverse groups of people, she has adopted so much of black culture and has always honored other cultural groups.

I therefore listened to her in a bit of shock. Her words made me realize that historical and generational issues of injustice and discrimination in our society seem to appear and re-appear in conversations at the most inopportune times—such as when we are enjoying life at a coffee shop drinking a latte with our best friend. Although I knew that my friend was not trying to disrespect me with her questions and comments, I immediately went into a default mode of silence, assuming that no matter how I explained things, she wouldn't get it. And I didn't feel like going into a conversation about Black Lives Matter, All Lives Matter, or anything else that would potentially matter. I wanted to talk about cruises and fun. I didn't want to talk about journeys I had not been a part of and organizations I did not establish.

But after prolonged silence between the two of us, I had an aha moment. She was pretty much saying the same thing to me that I have been feeling for a while each time someone asks me a question about the present state of racial and cultural divides in our nation. People have asked me ques-tions that I can't explain, or have expected me to be the spokesperson for the entire black culture or other ethnic com-munities. I have felt that I was being drawn into societal issues and cultural divides that I have no responsibility for and that are out of my control. My friend was similarly expressing her pain from the behaviors and words of people who did not take the time to get to know her individually in the true context of

17

who she really is, and who have also attached her color and ethnicity to the present ills of society.

I knew that the only answers I could share would have to be ones in which I could shed a bit of light about injustices that have occurred in our society due to unequal power structures and the dishonoring of people. But I also knew that the conversation would have to end with the truth that Jesus has given to us in Romans 12:1-2: that we are not to conform to the patterns of this world, even in how we respond to adversity and conversations that stretch us.

I told my friend that we don't have a skin problem but rather a sin problem. The root of the problems of division in our society are mainly because people need to have a relationship with Jesus. My answer felt like a safe response. But then my friend responded, "That's true, but we also have some Christians who are prejudiced."

I didn't think she would understand or care about my journey, but I decided to share anyway. And as I shared more and more with her, she did get it and she did care. In the process I realized that the conversation was not just about my pain but also about me gaining a greater understanding of what she was trying to communicate without getting offended. I, too, listened and grasped better the layers behind her words. Thankfully, we had already established a relationship with each other based on vulnerability and transparency, so we could safely share our pain and joys without feeling judged.

Similar themes of unity and diversity came up recently in a conversation I was in with a group of leaders. People wanted to know how we could become more intentional in connecting with minorities in the community. I was quiet during most of the conversation because I could tell that others around the table were becoming frustrated.

Someone said, "Why do we need to talk about diversity? There is only one race—the human race. I am not a racist and I love everyone. I don't see color, and we should be talking about advancing the kingdom of God and not race and diversity issues. We are creating more issues by talking about these things." I was asked what my thoughts were, and when I didn't respond, someone said, "I don't see you as a black woman. You are just like us." Of course, I understood what they meant, and I knew that my new friends meant no disrespect, but it was a great time to help them understand that it is okay to celebrate the beauty of diversity. It's okay to see color and yet not make skin color the basis of how we connect with people. I explained to them, as I have before, that they *do* see my color and that it's okay to celebrate God's creation and let people be themselves. And I affirmed that talking about ways to bring people from different backgrounds together is indeed okay.

These conversations reminded me that topics such as history and diversity and division will keep coming up, and that they can cause deep hurt or be a pathway to deeper understanding, depending on how we respond.

Listening to Learn About the Experiences of Others

Our present society is full of headline stories and subliminal messages about racial, ethnic, and socioeconomic divisions. We hear about the polarization of people according to what they have or don't have, political preferences, and other differences. They're the stories we would all just rather ignore and hope would go away—but they don't. They linger on the news channels, get likes on social media, get tweeted over and over again, and pop up in our workplaces and places of worship. And because our personal histories and experiences, as well as the histories of our cultural groups, are different, we interpret and understand these stories differently. For example, one person saying that some injustices no longer exist does not negate the fact that the word *exist* means something different to other people, based on what they have personally experienced in society and what constitutes a dishonoring, dehumanizing experience to them.

Intentional and unintentional offenses across cultural lines have existed since Adam and Eve sinned in the Garden of Eden. It can be easy for us to try to dismiss a person's journey because we don't understand it or to think that we can't build a relationship with someone unless we agree about everything. The reality is that we are not necessarily going to agree about many things because, again, we experience the world differently and face different challenges from each other. And relationships and perceptions we have today have been deeply affected by our different histories, even though people we meet now didn't live during the era of institutional slavery or may not have been born during Jim Crow laws or other horrible acts of injustice in history. Most of my white friends say to me that they really feel like they are being blamed for everything unjust that has happened in our society in the past, whether it is slavery, segregation, or any historical context of racism and prejudice. Many other individuals or groups of people in our society still experience present-day institutional discriminations and intentional acts of prejudice.

History has caused long-standing divisions that need to be broken down. When someone mentions to me that they are not the cause of any problem between different people or cultural groups going on in society right now, my response is that even though that might be true, if they are not being courageous by befriending people who they don't understand, then they are not helping to model a solution. Building rela-tionships with each other can help us get outside of ourselves and see the perspectives and experiences of others that are different from ours, and then lead us to find common ground that we wouldn't have thought existed between us. But how do we go about this?

We must practice empathetic learning and listening. This means being willing to listen in order to attempt to understand what someone is feeling or experiencing and to remind our-selves that one person's experience of situations and people is not the same as another's, instead of listening with the intent to reprimand or judge a person, or to rewrite their story with our version of it. We have to humble ourselves to truly listen and learn from each other. We also have to learn from our painful experiences and not allow them to harden our hearts against people, cause us to have a victim mentality, or miss opportunities to build new crosscultural friendships. We listen to the stories of others with the intent to learn. When we allow someone to be their authentic self and we remain our authentic self, we establish healthy relationships. We can't change or alter past pain that someone has experienced because it makes us feel uncomfortable.

Empathetic listening builds bridges to authentic relationships. Dismissing others' pain only increases our division and mistrust of each other. I recently heard someone express that he is tired of hearing people say that they are hurt. His response was, "Everyone has been hurt. I'm tired of hearing it." This attitude will never allow another to freely share about their pain. Similarly, when the words "they just need to get over it" are said to someone who has experienced some form of dishonor or disrespect from a person or group in another culture, mistrust is immediately ignited.

One of the hardest things for some people to deal with is the minimization or marginalization of their pain of being dishonored as a human being. Words such as "It's not that bad, and we don't want to talk about it," or agreeing that a situation was bad but declaring that it can only be discussed at the comfort level of others, cause emotional walls to be erected in relationships, rather than building bridges to wholeness.

Keeping our feelings bottled up can also feed mistrust. Unless we have relationships built on mutual trust and respect, awkward moments will occur in which we don't want to share with others what we really feel or believe because we fear that we might become an instant outsider to that person. This fear of damaging a friendship can lead us to merely smile and create invisible mental compartments for what we will and will not share with a person. The beauty of any genuine relationship is that what we say in hard conversations about life or what is happening in our society, or even what we say when we're expressing our true feelings, does not have to be taken as a personal insult but rather can be an opportunity to pursue mutual understanding.

All relationships will be tested, given that we have had such different experiences in life, and at some point we just have to make a decision that we will allow the transforming work of Jesus to keep our hearts soft and help us continue to display love. It is helpful to pray right in the midst of hard conversations and ask Jesus to use your encounter with the person positively to help rewrite their narrative of mistrust.

The day at the coffee shop with my friend is one I will never forget. I watched her move through the emotions of anger, pain, and then fear that her comments had truly offended me

23

and perhaps breached the trust in our relationship. It was also the moment when I knew God was speaking to my heart about me playing a key role in pointing her to the truth about Jesus and the life that he modeled while here on earth. In addition, it was a special opportunity to speak truthfully with her about why there is so much mistrust among some people of color toward the white race. For example, I told her about firms that provided meals to passengers at railroad stations in the past. They were prohibited from serving meals to white passengers and passengers of color in the same room, at the same counter, or at the same table; the penalty for doing so was a fine ranging from twenty-five dollars to a hundred dollars or imprisonment for up to thirty days. She, in turn, explained to me why some white people have also developed mistrust toward different racial groups. I shared how, even if it's not the best way to relate to others, historical pain can be the framework through which some people see and treat other cultures. And I explained that, even though my life in Christ gives me a different blueprint for and perspective on how I should treat all people whether I agree with them or not, everyone has to allow God to do the personal work of healing and truth-telling in their lives.

My friend and I were able to have a hard conversation that day about racism, dishonor, and cultural differences because we have a relationship based on transparency and vulnerability with each other that we have cultivated throughout the years. We have learned to listen to each other and pray for each other. I realized a bit later in the day that I should not have viewed my friend's questions as an interruption in our time together but rather as a gift from God that allowed us to learn more about each other and to share both tears and joy through our stories.

I can honestly say that our conversation that day, during which we both had to release the need to be right and genuinely listen to each other and wait in the presence of Jesus to hear what he would say to each of us, has deepened our relationship in a beautiful way.

The big subsets of prejudice—racism (prejudice based on race or ethnicity), sexism, classism, and prejudice based on religion—are always before us and don't seem to go away. Sometimes we are torn about all of these things, but we don't have to be torn apart. We can't isolate ourselves from these issues, but we can try to build bridges with diverse people through employing empathetic learning and listening. Most heart changes are truly tested in a struggle, and when we allow Jesus to show us how we might be the instrument of healing for someone else, we don't see their pains as trivial but rather as a place where we can connect over our common humanity. All it takes sometimes is one positive interaction with someone from a different culture to learn to trust a new person or group.

Healing Historical Hurts Through Racial Righteousness

While writing this book I had the privilege of being part of an event called Journey to Racial Righteousness. I had heard the term *racial righteousness* before and thought that it was similar to racial reconciliation, which is bringing to light the truth that the finished work of Jesus on the cross has made us all one. Racial righteousness, I learned, deals deeply with the inner working of our hearts by addressing the biblical, ethical, and moral issues of how we treat each other.

When I was invited to take part in this journey of racial righteousness with four other churches coming together over one weekend, I was beyond elated. The thought of having a place to share honestly and vulnerably, build new relationships, be listened to in an accepting environment, and of finally having a forum for spiritual growth was just as delightful to me as a piece of crispy fried chicken!

The purpose of the weekend was to learn from each other as we wrestled with the issue of racial righteousness and the godly response to ethnic and racial divisions. We wanted to share our fears and hope in a safe environment where the Spirit of God could lead us and our emotions into truth about his heart for all people.

We began the journey all together in one large room, but we were sitting with people we already knew. It was the safe thing to do. However, it meant that the start of the two-day journey was a bit stagnant for me. The lectures on diversity and biblical insights were the necessary foundation for our time together, but by the end of that first day it looked like the weekend was going to be a surface-only experience because no one wanted to offend anyone. It was similar to some of the trainings I had facilitated in the past in which I wanted to keep it safe, inoffensive, and just get through the time with minimal confrontation. After careful conversations about division in the church, we all politely stood in line for our lunch, barely speaking to each other.

It was not until the second day of our journey to racial righteousness that our group *really* took a journey together. We were placed in smaller groups, and a Hispanic man sitting next to me at my table broke down in tears in front of us when he received a phone call during our lunch time. He came back to the group table after his phone call with tears still running down his cheeks. Just a few minutes into his weeping, everyone at the table got up from their chairs without any prompting or words and surrounded him, offering prayers, hugs, and some measure of comfort without knowing what the situation was that had brought so much pain to him. He then shared with us about the recent personal loss of his wife and how the phone call had ignited pain afresh. We didn't ask him to give us details of the phone call because we knew that his pain had touched all of us in some way.

Before the tears from this man started, my experience at the table had been one of being with a group of seven people who had said very little to each other, and thus there had been very few steps toward transforming into a caring, compassionate community. Our journey up to that point had not had any real relational aspect; it was only once we connected over similar stories of pain that transformation began to occur.

Even though the situation was different from the one this man had experienced, my experience of the cancer-related death of my husband moved me from talking to a Hispanic male (who I actually thought was white) about being a black woman on a journey, to a spiritual sojourner sharing in pain with a fellow traveler in life. Through the shared experience of pain and brokenness, I came to realize that the greatest journey with anyone is the journey of compassion, understanding, and empathy, which can only happen when individuals are transparent with each other.

When we move closer in transparency and vulnerability to those we fear or even feel uncomfortable around, we can share our difficult experiences while creating a safe environment that allows us to dive deep into hard conversations. In my group that day, we weren't thinking about whether we should call him Hispanic, Mexican, or Latino. After his tears and sharing, our time and focus shifted to how Jesus has transformed our pain and forged in us a greater sense of dependency on the Lord. We found that our true journey with each other had nothing to do with the color of our eyes and hair but with the invisible connection of our hearts. Our personal relationship with Jesus was the catalyst and motive for wanting to build community with each other. And our journey of racial righteousness began on the day we let our guard down with each other. Since then we have remained in touch with each other. And yes, we did talk about historical injustices, too, but not from a place of just talking about problems. Instead, we focused on solutions that could begin with us at that table together.

We can no longer choose to stay in our comfort zones and believe that real spiritual transformation will still take place in our hearts or that our character will be formed more and more into the likeness of Christ. If our everyday encounters are only with people who always think the same way we do, eat the same foods, read the same books, and embrace life the same way we do, we are not being stretched and formed into the ultimate image of Christ.

Pause Moment

- What effects do you think feeling the continued pain of systemic racial and ethnic discrimination can have on a person? Are the conversations uncomfortable for you, or do you engage courageously as a learner and at times a teacher? Explain.

- Do you feel that the playing field is equal for all people? Why or why not?

- If a person from a different cultural group pointed out to you that one of your comments was offensive to them, how would you respond at the time? Would it change the likelihood of you making a similar comment in the future? Why or why not?

- Revisit the definition of Ubuntu and write in your own words what it means to you about building a diverse community of friends.

cultural identity and biases

Without dignity, identity is erased. In its absence, men
are defined not by themselves, but by their captors
and the circumstances in which they are forced to live.

LAURA HILLENBRAND

In the 1940s, two black psychologists who were married to each other, Kenneth and Mamie Clark, were instrumental in the civil rights movement, conducting important research about the effects of race and segregation using experiments that were called "the doll tests." The doll tests consisted of placing a white doll and a black doll in front of black children and asking them to choose the doll they thought was the prettiest, nicest, and other "best" qualities. Overwhelmingly, the black children chose the white dolls and said it was because they were the most beautiful.

The data collected contributed to the ruling by the US Supreme Court that school segregation was illegal. According to Chief Justice Earl Warren in the *Brown v. Board of Education* opinion, "To separate them from others of similar age and qualifications solely because of their race generates a feeling of inferiority as to their status in the community that may affect their hearts and minds in a way unlikely to ever be undone."

If I had participated in the doll test in 1975 when I was in high school—which was a turning point in my life about my identity—I would have also chosen the white doll because I, too, had a feeling of inferiority based on my flawed internal identity. There was nothing intriguing about a black doll that symbolized one thing for me: struggle.

I grew up in predominately black hoods (neighborhoods) in inner-city Chicago and Gary, Indiana. My neighborhoods were a bit diverse, with a few Hispanic people and people from the Middle East, but very few white people. And yet I pretty much watched all-white television shows such as *Leave It to Beaver*, *Wonder Woman*, and *Father Knows Best*, and I listened to white musicians such as the Beatles and my favorite, Elvis Presley. I know there is nothing wrong with enjoying different genres of shows, music, and the like. My point is that my identity was flawed in that I didn't see the value of who God created me to be. I would tell all of my friends that I wanted to marry Elvis, and I believed that I would never have a good life or enjoy the American Dream unless I was white. In truth, I didn't really know what the American Dream was supposed to be, but I felt that the American Nightmare was relived over and over again in my neighborhood. I ignorantly believed that white people were the real enemy even though the paradox is that I wanted to emulate white culture.

Growing up I didn't have a relationship with Jesus, but I remember when I prayed for the first time in my life: on April 4, 1968, after the assassination of Dr. Martin Luther King Jr. I was a young girl at the time, but when the news report came of his death, I dropped to my knees by the side of my bed, sobbing and shaking. Fear enveloped me then that I was doomed to a life of despair because my fearless leader had died and no one would protect me from the evil people in the world who, again, I thought were white people. I earnestly prayed that God would make me a white girl. In my naivety I remember saying to him, "If you make me white, I won't tell anyone that you made a mistake. I will even love black people if you change my skin color." While it seems so foolish now, I was sincere in my request.

As I was on my journey of understanding my own identity and cultural biases, the life of a French girl named Louise intersected with mine in my third-period speech class. She walked into our classroom—which was all-black except for the teacher and one Hispanic boy—and sat in the front of the class by invitation of the teacher. Wearing a big smile and a brightly colored dashiki, she also sported blond dreadlocks down to her waist.

Our class had just started a lively conversation about our next debate when Louise walked in. It became quiet, and I knew that the other students were wondering why she was invited to sit in the front of the class by our teacher, who was white. Someone made the comment, "Can we ever have a place that's just our place without the invasion of white people? I get sick and tired of white girls trying to act like they are black!" That someone was me, which is why I remember the rude comment. Of course, I was reprimanded by the teacher, who thought it was a very insensitive comment and respectfully stated that I needed to apologize, which I did.

At some point, though, Louise and I became best friends. I honestly don't remember what caused the shift. But I knew that she and I were both were grappling a bit with who we were— me more than her. Our friendship ignited a bit of a revolt by some of my friends at the high school, who began to use the terms *sell-out*, *Oreo*, and *Uncle Tom* directed toward me.

Louise stayed at the school for an entire year and never stopped wearing her dreadlocks and African clothes. I found out that the reason she wore so many African garments is because her Dad had brought them back from a missions trip he went on to Kenya. She explained to me that she was not trying to be black and that she would not stop wearing her dreadlocks because she had finally gotten to a place of accepting herself without tying her life to others' expectations.

Louise was also unique in that I never heard her say anything bad about anyone who talked about her, and she would always say that she was praying for them. She talked about Jesus with a joy that was intriguing to me. I surrendered my life to the Lord the year before I graduated high school, and I know that God allowed Louise and me to intersect so that I could get to know Jesus and his love through the love that she showed to me.

When Louise eventually transferred to another school, I experienced deep sadness in my heart, though I also experienced joy over her unselfish behavior. My attitude changed and I became a young woman of compassion and empathy toward others. So many students at the school missed the opportunity to relate to her as a beautiful soul and to get to know her. She made some friends besides me, but she was pretty much an outsider. I am convinced that if she had been given the chance to be a friend to some of the students at the school, they could have become richer individuals on so many levels.

I once read a quote by businessman Max De Pree that reminds me of Louise and of how so much of what we believe about ourselves and others is rooted in not being able to both give and receive: "We need to give each other the space to grow, to be ourselves, to exercise our diversity. We need to give each other space so that we may both give and receive such beautiful things as ideas, openness, dignity, joy, healing, and inclusion."

Whether we want to admit it or not, many times our cultural upbringing and the lens through which we view others can lead to limited relational connections with people from diverse backgrounds. But in looking at culture from a Christian

35

perspective, submitting ourselves to the lordship of Christ changes our human relationships and how we view others, as well as how we treat each other.

I spent my teen years and most of my young adult life in the Black Power movement even though I envied being white, hating the very thought of living in a world with people who would never understand the meaning of white privilege (that there are some things certain white people have inherited just because of skin color). This led me to curiously follow a movement called White Privilege—a predominately white group that included top authors and motivational speakers. This group traveled to universities and cities, giving presentations about privilege in our society.

At some point during my connection to the White Privilege group, however, I personally started hating the words *white privilege*. The concept refers to societal privileges that benefit white people beyond what is commonly experienced by non-white people. It started feeling wrong for me to be connected to a movement that was bringing so much mistrust and confusion.

At one point in my life I went through dire financial hardship that included homelessness. I found myself standing in line with people of all ethnicities who were trying to get food stamps, rental assistance, and any other help that would allow us to survive. I always noticed that most of the people standing in line with me during the wee hours of the morning were white. What was I to do with that reality?

Conversations about benefits and entitlement among the less fortunate are not the most pleasant, but when I have connected with people who have been going through similar challenging experiences as myself, we don't create a name or label to put on it. We have just seen ourselves as fellow travelers who are continually learning how to connect with each other with compassion and empathy. These encounters have brought healing and correction to the way I view others.

Each time I would try to submit that part of my self-identity to the lordship of Jesus, another situation would occur that let me know I was not fully healed. My greatest moment of heart change occurred in the most unusual way, during a time when I applied for a national position at a firm. I was one of three candidates being considered for a high-ranking management role. The person who interviewed me, however, told me that I would probably not get the position because I didn't have blond hair and blue eyes. Once again I was thrown into a pit of dismay about my cultural self-identity and came face-to-face with the reality that I was not yet fully able to see my value, worth, and dignity as a human being created in the image of God. Although it was graciously explained to me that some of the clients wouldn't relate to a black woman in such a key position, I knew that Jesus was trying to get a message across to me. It wasn't the message of the prayer that I had prayed earlier about changing my identity, though. Rather, it was a message that I needed to celebrate and embrace the fact that dignity was already given to me when I entered the world. I learned that when I could fully accept who I was, I could also accept others without feeling that I had to compete with or compare myself to anyone.

Vicki and Me: A Tale of Friendship

Another story from when I was growing up provides a joyful and beautiful glimpse of what genuine friendship can look like when it is rooted in love, loyalty, and a strong sense of connection between two persons, despite the outward and cultural differences that exist between them.

In the United States during the 1970s, there was a strong sense of "us versus them" among different ethnic and cultural groups. But my friend (a teenage white girl who had been judged as not valued by her own white culture) and I (a black girl who had been transplanted from my predominantly black community) found ourselves connected to each other because neither of us felt accepted, understood, or validated in our high school. Drawn together by this mutual feeling of being peripheral to our school culture and our vulnerability of being excluded not only from our peers but also because of some presumed unacceptable cultural and ethnic trait, we released our fears of each other and developed a wonderful friendship. Because of our strong bond, we felt more like sisters of the heart than friends.

We each felt our own appreciation and gratitude for the other for different reasons, but ultimately for the same reason: we had found someone we could relate to with compassion and respect despite our cultural and ethnic differences. We were both truly grateful that we had found a true friend who was graced with tolerance, compassion, and a worldview that included the value of all people. And we believed that it was okay to truly be ourselves (*I am*) and build genuine community with each other (*we are*). In addition, we realized that without each other, our character would not have been as enriched as it was in walking together. These two teenage girls were able to transcend potential barriers—like being intolerant and unwilling to pursue understanding beyond the surface—that could have prevented them from being enriched by each other's friendship.

Even though we don't all have the same background, we all have the same face—the face of a human being—and our stories are connected through everyday ordinary life encounters.

Pause Moment

- If you had to identify with a person in this chapter, who would it be, and why?

- Reflect on the following passages: 1 John 1:12 and Isaiah 61:3, 10. How do we learn to live out of our new identity?

■ Explore your own cultural identity. How would you describe who you are and where you fit? If someone does not see or feel they are a person of worth, can it influence how they view others? Explain.

lessons in humility

The true way and the sure way to friendship is through humility—being open to each other, accepting each other just as we are, knowing each other.

MOTHER TERESA

Intensely jet-lagged and groggy, when I stepped off the plane shortly after midnight I was honestly terrified! I was at Noi Bai International Airport in Hanoi, Vietnam. The year was 2005.

I had traveled over twenty hours on two planes with more than three hundred people who did not look like me and most of whom did not speak English. Even before I arrived, though, shortly after my takeoff with Korean Airlines from Los Angeles, I had asked myself what in the world I had been thinking to agree to guest lecture at Hanoi University in Vietnam.

An organization had first approached me earlier that year and offered me an opportunity to go to Vietnam with a team of professionals who would spend a couple of weeks teaching various topics and engaging with the Vietnamese Chamber of Commerce. I was a bit skeptical—yet also excited. I believed it would be a wonderful opportunity to teach diversity and human resource management at such a prestigious university as Hanoi University, but I immediately went to the race question. Specifically, *Are there any black people working in Vietnam*? A friend asked me if it really mattered whether there were any black people in Vietnam, and I responded, "Well, yeah, kinda. I'm just being honest! I just wonder if I will be an odd spectacle in a country that fought a war with America and probably has no frame of reference for black people." My friend laughingly said, "You are an odd spectacle in any country—even here in the United States!"

I had traveled to Ethiopia and Kenya for short missions trips in the years prior to the offer of teaching in Vietnam, and I somehow believed that my mission in life was to go back to the motherland of Africa—not the "other land" of Vietnam. Once I knew I had been given the green light by God to go to Vietnam, however, I was elated at learning about a culture that was so foreign to me—or so I thought.

As I gathered my luggage from the carousel at the airport in Vietnam, I saw a plethora of people standing in the waiting section ready to greet people as they walked through the gates. I didn't know who would be meeting me at midnight, except maybe a taxi driver. A young man and woman waiting with a cart full of colorful flowers briefly caught my attention, and I thought, *There are nice people here at midnight smiling and waiting for someone with* a lot *of flowers in that cart!* But why would I think that there would *not* be nice people in Vietnam? Probably because I had honestly built a stereotype in my mind of an entire culture of people based on only one frame of reference—the Vietnam War. I knew nothing much about the Vietnam War, and I knew even less about the people who reside in Vietnam.

When I walked through the gates where people were waiting, the couple with the cart full of flowers came toward me smiling and holding a sign that said, "Welcome MelindaJoy!" Wow! It was the dean of the university and one of the professors from where I would be teaching. My drive from the airport to my residence was not very long, but the kindness I experienced in the taxi with two complete strangers was amazing! The dean would later become one of my best friends. I believe that there are times when we really don't meet strangers—just friends who are waiting for us. They helped me feel that I belonged.

My initial interaction with my now best friend and the professor was a glimpse into a culture of honor, respect, and love that I would never forget and would continue to experience during my next five trips to Vietnam over the course of six years. It was not the flowers in the cart that stole my heart, though; it was the unconditional love that I have been given from the heart of a people group that I would have never believed would accept me. Interestingly, building friendships

43

has not been difficult or strained because my friendships have been built on nothing less than honor on both sides. And I absolutely love Vietnam now! I love the people and the country. I enjoy eating crepes for dessert, as the French influence is evident in the food choices, architecture, and culture of Hanoi. I also love eating pho—the popular Vietnamese noodle soup. The tree-lined streets and beautiful lakes have soothed my soul and are a wonderful reminder to me of the many ways I can miss the beauty around me if I only allow myself to see beauty through the lens of what I am accustomed to defining as beautiful.

Crosscultural Challenges

This is not to say that I never faced crosscultural challenges in my travels to Vietnam. My experiences there have been both exciting and frustrating because I have had to learn how to serve as a leader and not position myself above the culture. From the curious stares and giggles of students at the university to the blatant stares of people in the streets who wondered why I was shopping at the markets in Hanoi or running around a lake doing tai chi in the morning with a group of seniors, I knew it was because they didn't have a frame of reference for my presence in the city. It also took me some time to move beyond my comfort zone. During my first visit to Vietnam, for example, I frequented more of the restaurants that cater to Americans with hamburgers and french fries. It was comfortable to eat in places where I could order from the menu and not have to ask someone to help me order a meal.

During my second visit, however, I decided to initiate friendships in the country that I came to love—to step into the uncomfortable place of exploring new things and immerse myself in the culture of Vietnam. I started eating in places I would not have gone to during my first visit and trusted my new friends to let me enter into their intimate world with vulnerability and respect. This landed me in one of my most humiliating and yet useful learning experiences while in Hanoi, when some of my students decided to fix a special dinner for me.

I was so excited for the evening, but as we arrived at the beautiful village where my students lived and I started walking through the maze of homes in tight quarters, I had a full-blown panic attack. I began feeling trapped in the semidark, winding crevices of the village. My heart started racing and I found myself hyperventilating.

My students could only speak limited English at the time, and I could only speak limited Vietnamese. When I stopped and tried to explain to them that I needed to get air, they surrounded me and began hugging me and holding my hand, which literally made me feel even more panicky. Being unable to explain fully what was happening to me caused me to start crying. I tried to pull away from the two students on either side of me only to have them hold my hand closer. Although I was

45

a bit embarrassed, at that moment I realized I was indeed in a foreign country and dependent on the mercy of the people there and the friendships I had begun to form.

One of my students realized that I was experiencing deep fear and decided that they should take me to the opening in the village where I could see. They walked me back to the opening and consoled me. Then they tried to walk me back in. During this attempt to get me to the home where the meal was waiting, the word spread throughout the village that the American professor was in a panic mode and couldn't explain why. Some of the curious residents peeked out of their windows to view the commotion, and the most interesting thing happened: individuals came out of their homes and began walking alongside me.

Believe it or not, I made it to the home where my special dinner and hosts were waiting. Honestly, I cried all the way, feeling that I was suffocating while my friends and strangers held my hands. It was now dark and very warm, and I prayed that God would help me. I arrived to smiling faces, and my hosts started clapping when they saw me. The amount of food prepared for me was touching! But the panic returned when I sat down with so many people surrounding me. What should have been a one-hour visit ended up being more than three hours.

The evening ended with my hosts assuring me that they did not feel bad about their experience with me and they were still excited about fixing a meal for me. Through this very humbling experience, God began to show me the fear that I had silently carried for over a year whenever I was in a new situation, especially in a country I was still getting accustomed to. But rather than judging me, my hosts said it was good to see me being transparent. This was the *second* time over a period of months that I had to be rescued.

My first rescue came when I traveled to underground caves with a group of professors from Hanoi. The day started out on a high, joyful note, but as the residents of Hanoi began to crowd into the underground caves, I began to feel claustrophobic and had to be dragged out of the cave due to my fainting and inability to walk. My rescue by a ten-year-old in a paddle boat was another humiliating experience for me. As a result, my students and colleagues in Vietnam gained another perspective of me as a human being with weaknesses, flaws, and the need for a lot of grace. I concluded that I honestly like to be in control of my situations, surroundings, and circumstances.

When we are not in control, especially in a new culture, we are stretched to be authentic and open, which allows others to learn from us. There is no substitute for experience. The same virtues of empathy, compassion, and understanding are present in all cultures.

I traveled back to Vietnam many times after the panic attacks occurred. My personal application about these situations is that my friends needed to see there is not a big gap between being a fearful American in an unfamiliar Vietnamese village and a panicking Vietnamese riding a subway for the first time in New York (which happened to a friend). I continually allow myself to learn from people of different racial and cultural groups in America—someone who might be sitting in a cubicle across from me at work or the person in my neighborhood who I could smile at or say hello to. And this continues to take humility and vulnerability.

The words *transparent* and *vulnerable* are sometimes used interchangeably, but I like to define *transparent* as "honest and free of deceit" and *vulnerable* as "being open yet susceptible to emotional injury." Everyone is at different levels in their ability to deal with racial and ethnic issues, and each person is also susceptible to emotional injury while trying to befriend someone from a different culture. One of the greatest pains that can occur is when a person bears their soul to someone or tries to help someone, only to be rejected. My encouragement in these types of situations is to remember that ignorance about certain cultural norms is cured rather quickly, but arrogance will take a bit longer to both address and cure.

In 2 Corinthians 6:11-13, the apostle Paul gives an invitation to the Corinthian church to step into a life of openness with God and each other:

Dear, dear Corinthians, I can't tell you how much I long for you to enter this wide-open, spacious life. We didn't fence you in. The smallness you feel comes from within

48

you. Your lives aren't small, but you're living them in a small way. I'm speaking as plainly as I can and with great affection. Open up your lives. Live openly and expansively! (*The Message*)

Opportunities for Connection

I believe that God really does prepare us in so many ways for our connections with different people before we meet them, and I was being prepared in Colorado Springs for my journey in Vietnam. Years before my first trip to Vietnam, I was immersed in Vietnamese culture in my own city.

In 1997 after the death of my husband, I moved into a small efficiency apartment in Colorado Springs and was immediately befriended by a young Vietnamese couple who lived in the building. The husband was a chef at a local hotel and his wife was a beautician. I spoke no Vietnamese and they both spoke limited English—just enough to communicate with me. But I knew there was a specific reason for our mutual exchange of smiles each time we saw each other in the hallway.

Then an opportunity for a deeper connection happened! The Vietnamese beautician cared about me even though we couldn't understand each other's language. But I understood the language of the heart, which were meals cooked for me, groceries picked up for me, and evidence of care and love. She asked me if she could style my hair with a curling iron so she could get some practice with black hair. As nice as she was, I told her no, politely explaining that black hair is not like Asian hair and that I could potentially lose a lot of hair if she did something wrong. And then I would have to get extensions or do something else with my hair. In her very sweet way, she said okay, but every time she saw me she would say in her beautiful broken English, "I do your hair," and show me her certificate from cosmetology school to assure me that she was capable. Eventually I decided to give her a chance, figuring that there was not a lot of damage she could do with a curling iron. And I wanted to get to know her better.

When I arrived at her apartment with my curling iron, I found that she and her husband had cooked a big meal for me to introduce me to foods from Vietnam. All went pretty well regarding the hair until she twisted the curling iron the wrong way and could not get it out of my hair while it was hot. I was able to get it out with only a few strands of hair coming out with the comb. But what happened afterward in our relationship was so phenomenal that it was worth having the journey with the curling iron.

I think that out of some remorse for the hair situation she and her husband decided they owed me meals every day. I assured them that they didn't, but we somehow came to an agreement that they would teach me how to speak Vietnamese, and I would teach them English—with the Bible. Our times together were rich in friendship. They taught me about their culture by showing me videos about Vietnam and explaining the meaning of Vietnamese songs. The three of us went to the Vietnamese community in Denver to try different restaurants. I didn't give much thought to what was really taking place in our relationship: Jesus had brought the nations to me—in my own backyard. Of course, I didn't know that I would eventually visit Vietnam.

I believe my Vietnamese friends were brought into my life by divine direction, and although neither one accepted the Lord as their personal Savior during our time together, I believe God used me to plant seeds for the gospel. And I trust that others came along to water those seeds until the time when God ultimately brought a harvest. They eventually moved out of the building and it was hard to keep in touch, but I know God brought them into my life for many reasons—and one of those reasons was to prepare me for my first trip to Vietnam in 2005.

Will You Love Me When I'm in America?

I have always come back to America feeling empty with a yearning to go back to Vietnam, but in 2013 Jesus began to show me how many times he has put Vietnamese people in my path in Colorado and the opportunities I have missed to build relationships in my city and neighborhood.

I remember showing a man a picture of my friends in Vietnam as we were sitting at a table eating together. He said to me with all sincerity, "How do I know these pictures were not taken in a nail shop here in the US?" He thought his comment was funny, but it ignited my heart's desire to connect with the large Vietnamese community where I live in Colorado Springs. I began to answer a question that someone posed to me in a very transparent, noncondemning way—a question that has guided me in my being intentional both here in America and across the waters: "Will you still love me when I am in America and not overseas?"

As I began to do research on the Vietnamese culture in Colorado, I realized that within a three-mile radius of my residence there are at least six Vietnamese restaurants and three churches. In addition, across the street from me is a huge salon owned by people from Cambodia and Vietnam. I have started being intentional about learning the names of people who are in my neighborhood, listening to their stories of acclimating to America, learning new phrases in Vietnamese, and sharing about my friends and experiences in Vietnam, which always ignites smiles and lively conversations. I realized that while I can love my friends in Vietnam and other places overseas, I am also asked to love people from different cultural and ethnic groups in my city.

It's not always easy to be open with people or unmask ourselves in front of those we walk with—both overseas and in our own neighborhoods. It is a big risk. But if we are honest with God and ourselves, we can learn to be honest with one another. Then we can see one another as the Lord sees us: people with value, worth, and deserving of respect.

First Thessalonians 1:5 states, "You know how we lived among you for your sake." This Scripture relates to being culturally aware and sensitive, understanding someone different from us while leaving our comfort zone to relate to others.

Paul's passion drove him to leave his culture and comfort zone to live among those in a Macedonian city for "their sake." When Paul did this, they could see the power of God through human words and actions expressed with deep convictions. Like Paul, we must have a go-to versus a come-to attitude. To go to or cross over to another culture, even in our city or perhaps one seat over in our church, means that we daily live physically, emotionally, socially, and spiritually with an expectation that opportunities are always present to connect with someone new and perhaps present the gospel of Jesus.

Pause Moment

■ How are you contributing to the communities of which you are a part? Do these communities include different racial and ethnic groups? Has someone from another culture first initiated a relationship with you? Describe that person. What does it mean to live among those in another culture, even if in your community or neighborhood?

- Assumptions about different cultural groups can be dangerous. How do you maintain your values and beliefs while being open to new ideas and new ways of doing things?

- How do you practice humility in your relationships with individuals from different cultures?

the bible and diversity

4

*Isn't it amazing that we are all made in God's image,
and yet there is so much diversity among his people?*
DESMOND TUTU

My heart's desire and passion is to see diverse cultural relationships that are healthy and beautiful images of Jesus' love for all people. And I believe that real transformation in the context of appreciating culture and building long-lasting crosscultural relationships is possible through simply embracing both similarities and differences.

If we are going to connect with people from diverse backgrounds, we need to practice the clear kingdom principles of righteousness, justice, love, and faithfulness. True servants lead and serve others with justice. We won't be able to connect immediately with every person we meet from another culture because it takes time, commitment, and courage, but it is worth the effort to push beyond all barriers that may exist on either side. Most relationships are formed naturally by spending time together and entering into another person's world through acts of kindness, respect, and prayer.

Jesus is the greatest model of how to serve others with respect. He didn't despise differences but rather taught us how to see others as valuable. He exercised humility, willingly gave up his rights and privileges, and became a servant of all. He treated all people with equal respect and dignity, often breaking with the traditions and customs of his day to do so.

Throughout his mission on earth, Jesus rejected false perceptions of others and intentionally crossed cultural barriers in order to love those he came in contact with. He restored the identity and dignity of all humans and invited them into a saving relationship with him.

An example of these principles is found in Jesus' encounter with the woman at the well (John 4:1-42). Jesus' behavior toward the woman transcended ethnicity, gender, culture, and her sinful background. Perhaps he purposefully selected this woman to illustrate that he values each of us. We tend to set up barriers, systems, and grids to define what is and is not socially acceptable. This Scripture illustrates that God sees each of us without using such grids. The fact that Jesus interacted with the Samaritan woman shows the high value he placed on her.

Jesus had many cultural and religious reasons to ignore this woman. She was a woman (v. 27), a Samaritan (v. 9), and had been married five times and was now living with a man who was not her husband (vv. 17-18). All of these factors would have put her outside of a Jewish man's orbit. Nevertheless, Jesus not only took the initiative to talk with her, but he also found common ground with her. He connected with her by admitting a basic need—thirst. We, too, can connect crossculturally by admitting our needs (e.g., need for directions, for food, for a friend, etc.).

When the woman arrived at the well, Jesus was on the woman's turf and began connecting with her by asking a question about water. Next, he moved the conversation from natural to spiritual water: to "a spring of water welling up to eternal life" (v. 14). He then revealed that he is the Messiah who was promised and that his ministry was for all people. He honored her with this revelation, which she accepted, and brought this good news to her people (vv. 39-42).

The Gospels are rich with daily encounters Jesus had with people—all kinds of people. The gospel message is not for a select group, rather Jesus desires that we share freely with every person, regardless of ethnic, cultural, or economic background (see Luke 4:16-21). No one is shown partiality. Jesus longs to have a relationship with each person.

Just as God loved us and sent his Son for our forgiveness, we need to love our neighbors and cross all cultural or language barriers with courage in order to love and share the good news with them.

Fear of the Unknown

We can become uncomfortable with the unknown. We must acknowledge that many times our fears are rooted in misinformation or the lack of information about a person. For instance, when I asked a friend why the white van in our neighborhood had bothered people, he stated, "No one else drives a van in our neighborhood." Fear of the unknown.

Depending on the context of any relational encounter, we can also make the mistake of viewing others only through the lens of what we are familiar with. In other words, in our initial interactions with people from different cultures, we often mentally attach what we deem as acceptable or unacceptable to their behaviors.

The kingdom of God is different, though, because it provides us with a new identity in which all people have value and worth regardless of their background, race, gender, and other characteristics. Remember the wristband WWJD (What Would Jesus Do)? I would love to design a new one that says WDJD (What Did Jesus Do). Jesus has already left us his model of how to relate to all people. Isn't it interesting that his approach to people of different backgrounds was to first establish the worth of each person? Jesus very intentionally allowed people to have an encounter with him that mirrored God's heart for all people and the availability of redemption.

We have to admit that we gravitate toward people who are like us. But many times we have more in common with people we perceive are different from us than we choose to believe. It is not just an issue of being able to relate to someone, though; we must also understand that when we connect with others, we should connect on equal footing. I believe God is calling believers to celebrate and not just tolerate each other. He wants us to look at the unconscious biases embedded in our hearts and be willing to go through the process of eradicating anything in our lives that does not honor Jesus.

Following Jesus

One of my favorite Bible illustrations of someone willing to go against the norms of society to befriend another based on love and forgiveness is found in the New Testament book of Philemon. It is a moving and profound letter written by the apostle Paul while he was imprisoned in Rome. Paul wrote to Philemon on behalf of Philemon's runaway slave Onesimus, who had stolen from him.

The apostle Paul not only asked Philemon to forgive his runaway slave but ultimately to receive Onesimus back into his home as an equal instead of a slave. It is interesting to note that Onesimus's name meant "useful," and yet Philemon may have seen him as useless. Applying this to our lives today, there are many people around us who are Onesimuses. It doesn't mean that they've done something wrong or sinned, but perhaps we have never seen them as persons of value and worth. Just as Paul writes and encourages Philemon to accept Onesimus as a brother in Christ, we followers of Christ also have opportunities to accept people from any background with a posture of love and acceptance.

Here's one way I've worked to apply Paul's letter to my life. As I travel and stay in hotels around the country, I am always amazed at the number of housekeepers who speak very little English. I've made an intentional effort to reach out to them by at least pausing and asking them how they are doing. It's my simple yet sincere attempt to communicate that they are useful beyond cleaning my bathroom.

Finally, a story that touches my heart so deeply and reflects how God values everyone equally is found in Acts 8:26-40—the story of the Ethiopian eunuch. Philip, a first-century evangelist, has been preaching in Samaria. As he travels he meets a eunuch on the road. From the story and from our knowledge of the times, we know that the eunuch was black (Ethiopian), a government official (we'd call him the Secretary of the Treasury), an accountant, and a castrated man who spent a considerable part of his life supervising a harem. He becomes a Christian and is baptized by Philip. Church history tells us that he became the head of the church in Africa.

This poses a question for us today: Can we, too, see each person that Jesus brings into our lives through his eyes of love? He did not care about the ethnicity, gender, or even the sin of the person who was in front of him. God is surprisingly at work in cultures other than our own, and we need to move out of our comfort zone for the sake of extending the gospel.

Pause Moment

- What Scriptures help you think about diversity?

- What was Jesus' attitude toward the Samaritan woman, and why do you think she listened to him?

- Since Jesus came to heal the brokenhearted and oppressed, how did he model that? What should our biblical response be today?

- Why do you think the eunuch responded so favorably to Philip in Acts 8? Who might be "passing by" that God has chosen for his purposes but doesn't fit your image of who God would choose to use?

PART TWO

practices
to express
dignity
and
compassion

pursue understanding in uncomfortable situations

The common denominator all Latinos have is that we want some respect. That's what we're all fighting for.

CRISTINA SARALEGUI

I believe there comes a point of time in our lives when we have an epiphany. Call it what we may—a life-changing encounter, a moment of reckoning, or many other things—but I call it the moment of getting real. When we think of building relationships with people who have different values and beliefs from our own or who are culturally different, we have to take a deep look inside our souls and be honest about what we see. It's like fog in a steam room. I love the sauna and steam room. It's my happy place—a place I frequent to relax and detox. But metaphorically, when we look at our souls, the very thing that's right in front of us can be foggy because we have foggy perceptions and foggy spiritual vision. We try to ignore or squeeze by the main thing occurring in our lives.

My mental fog was as thick as a cloud one day as I was sitting in the sauna at my local gym. When I walked into the space, nothing was unusual. Four quiet Korean women were already there. As I sat down, a conversation began, with each woman speaking in Hangul, the Korean dialect of North and South Korea.

I should say here that I sincerely love my neighborhood. It is a rich, beautiful mosaic of different cultures. We especially have a rich presence of Koreans, who own quite a few businesses in the community. Whether it's the local market where we get favorite exotic fruits and freshly baked desserts or the local cleaners where we get clothing alterations done, we live and work together with a respect for each other.

For some reason, however, on this day in the sauna I became increasingly agitated with the conversation. And while I didn't verbally say anything, my body language communicated agitation. I became so angry that I mentally constructed a top-ten list of how to get rid of distractions in the steam room.

I am thoroughly ashamed that it took me two minutes to develop a top-ten mental list of how to eliminate what I deemed distractions. It also took me every bit of one minute to shift my thinking after Jesus gently nudged my spirit to indicate that I was getting ready to head down a slippery slope of offense.

I believe that when we are honest about our emotions and feelings and let Jesus into the situation, he brings healing to us. He also gives us opportunities to immediately change our behavior when we are about to make cultural mistakes. I made a speedy decision in the steam room to totally alter my perspective by opening my eyes, looking at the women, and smiling with the biggest smile that I could muster. I decided to also just say hello and see what would happen. Turning to them, I said very slowly—taking almost three minutes to do so—"Hello, my name is MJ. What are your names?" To my amazement, one of the women turned to me, smiled, and responded, "Hey girlfriend, what's up? My name is Kanesha!" Kanesha! I nearly fell off the sauna seat and was thinking to myself, *How can you have a cultural name pretty much given to black women? Your name isn't Kanesha!* After talking with her though, I found out that Kanesha has a mother who is black and a Korean father.

I had assumed that I was going to get an answer back in broken English, and was therefore totally stunned at the response! Each of the women spoke English. When I asked them why they always spoke in their native language in the sauna, they explained that people at the gym were not friendly to them, so they had decided that one way to build community was to build it among themselves.

I really had to evaluate my heart on that day. It is amazing how one incident in our life, be it small or large, can alter the course and direction we are heading, either positively or negatively, and can cause us to totally reevaluate what we think and why we believe what we believe as it pertains to culture. Why had I found it so hard to love people in my neighborhood who are Korean American when I had been so excited to travel to Korea and spend time in Seoul previously? The result of my time in the sauna has been the development of close friendships with three of the women, especially Kanesha. We started taking exercise classes together and then would meet in the sauna to talk about recipes. Now we often laugh as we think back on my time of "anguish" and their perception of me as a snooty black woman.

Whether we want to admit it or not, culture really does play a part in how we relate to each other, and to say that racism and discrimination no longer exist in our society is to live in a place of denial. But as we look at culture from a Christian perspective, submitting ourselves to the lordship of Jesus Christ changes our human relationships, including how we view others and how we treat each other.

Connecting with Others Where They Are

During the past six years, I have spent time in Korea on my way to Vietnam to teach. It has made me realize that I have missed many opportunities to get to know the beauty of the Korean culture that exists in my neighborhood. Once again I have asked myself, *Will I still love any group of people when*

68

they are in America or American-born? The question applies not just to the Korean culture, of course, but to all people. I've wondered why in my neighborhood we have so many Korean- and Middle Eastern–owned black hair product shops that carry all of our favorite hair products and why business from the community is good, and yet we can't be friends with each other. We can buy and sell from each other but not speak to each other outside of the shops.

My conversations with the women in the steam room didn't immediately create deep friendships between me and any of them, but it was the beginning of a pleasant time of mini-conversations.

Jesus was very intentional about connecting with people where they were and allowing them to have an encounter with him that mirrored God's heart for all people and the ultimate plan of redemption for humankind.

Cultural Differences Don't Have to Separate Us

The message that our commonalities are the key to building vibrant relationships is the common thread throughout this book. However, this is not to say that cultural and ethnic dif- ferences don't matter. The term *melting pot* was very prom- inent during the 1970s and 1980s but meant little to my neighborhood. We did not like the term because we didn't want to "melt" who we were and had no desire to be figura- tively put in the "pot" with anyone we were not comfortable with or did not like. The notion of losing our distinctiveness as a people was unthinkable.

Some people thought of the melting pot analogy as putting an onion in a pot of stew to flavor it all. Others said that if the onion is put in a ziplock plastic bag before it's dropped in, it really does not flavor or enhance the stew. It just has the appearance of being in it. As an analogy, this view meant that some people would be totally allowed to be themselves while others would be the silent minority who lost their identity.

We had many churches in my neighborhood, and they were one of the places where we sought to protect our identity. We would allow anyone to come and visit for our Sunday services, but the people who visited that were not like us would always be visitors, encased in the ziplock bag labeled "not one of us." With amusement I would witness in my storefront Baptist church the response of the parishioners if an outsider would shout "Amen!" to an exhilarating Sunday morning sermon. The stares and hush would signal that an outsider had tried to become an insider without permission. After all, visitors must remain visitors and not pretend to be insiders unless invited. From a cultural perspective, assimilation—which means adopting the behaviors and cultural norms of another culture, especially a dominant one—represented to some the death of their heritage or identity.

In genuine relationships, cultures are not erased but should not be the basis of how we build relationships or what keeps us apart. People must feel that they can be their authentic selves and express their unique culture, background, and ethnicity while finding the commonalities that are the foundation for rich friendships. Often, though, those differences aren't what keep us apart; rather, it's our *fear* of our perceived differences.

Reflections from My Alley

As I was growing up in inner-city Chicago, I watched my neighborhood daily from my bedroom window, behind partially opened curtains. I noticed how different days in the alley from Monday through Saturday carried an unspoken color rule. On Sundays, most people were in church. The black Muslim kids in the neighborhood would not venture into the alley on the white day (the day all the white kids gathered to have fun), the few Asian kids, who were Korean, didn't play in the alley on the black day (the day the black kids played together), and no one who was not invited dared to be caught in the alley when it was not their day.

In addition, our neighborhood had small businesses and stores owned by Jews, and although we loved the services they offered to us, it was always "them" or "they" and never "we" or "us." My experiences with the Jewish people in the neighborhood were marked by my feeble, superficial attempts to make friends by saying things like, "I love the way you cook Polish sausages." The blank stares back at me were always an indication that I hadn't quite bridged the friendship gap with them by talking about kosher meats and Polish sausages without ever asking them how they were doing.

Each day I saw people of different races and cultures in my neighborhood standing at the *same* bus stop waiting for buses, shopping at the *same* neighborhood stores, crying over some of the *same* tragedies that happened nearby, sitting in some of the *same* movie theaters together and laughing at some of the *same* funny moments that occurred on the screen, applying for food stamps at the *same* welfare office, and dancing to some of the *same* music. In general, my neighborhood was full of people who really did a lot of the *same* things together. We would all dance at our block parties, but we always saw each other's differences and rarely any commonalities.

At the time I wondered how a neighborhood such as mine, which was so riddled by poverty and troubles, had so many people of other ethnicities living there. I consistently heard demeaning words to describe the racial groups represented. I didn't understand, though, why there were so many white people in my neighborhood who were poor just like the rest of us, and how Polish and Russian people ended up living in the inner-city projects along with black and Hispanic people. Little did I know at the time that it was a human element—our economic status—that brought all of us together in the same neighborhood. It could have been a point of connection for us.

But we ignored that fact in our continued quest to be different from each other.

I also noticed that our community was full of loving and caring people who borrowed sugar and soap from each other when money was tight and shared meals when food was scarce, but we somehow didn't understand that real community is formed in the trenches when we live, work, worship, and enjoy life together, beyond just meeting tangible needs. It's the concept of Ubuntu—connecting with people through shared life experiences. Words such as *culture*, *multicultural*, *multiracial*, and *diversity* weren't part of my vocabulary then, but I somehow knew that we were missing amazing opportunities to get to know each other through our similarities.

The Alleys We Find Ourselves In

An *alley* is a place in society that's off the beaten path. Many of us don't want to be there because it causes discomfort. Alleys are situations in which the choice we make could lead us closer to Ubuntu relationships or keep others at a distance. All of us know something about these situations. We don't talk about them openly, though, because they highlight the fact that there are unspoken rules of who we can build community with in society. It might be having to work next to someone from a different culture that we really don't like but figure it's only a nine-to-five situation. Or it could be sitting on an airplane next to someone and having our comfort disturbed when they speak a native language other than English; we feel a loss of control because we can't understand what they're saying.

Most people choose to go to the place where the path has already been carved, or, in simpler terms, to the people who may look different outwardly but who are easy for us to build relationships with because none of our assumptions or beliefs are being challenged. Or, when we can't avoid those different from us, we try to merely tolerate people instead of embracing them because we sometimes feel that our connection is temporary. But when a relational connection begins to be more than a temporary brief encounter and converges into our world and our worldview, discomfort begins. This is because both knowingly and unknowingly we have created customs and patterns that are really called "comfort zones" that merely mirror what society as a whole tells us is acceptable and unacceptable in how we relate to people. A comfort zone is a way of thinking that evolves from our unwillingness to move from what we believe or think we know to be true, to a place of excitement in adopting the heart of a learner. The customs of this world are designed to promote comfort, not community.

Here are a few examples of some of the unspoken "who we can be with" rules of society. The wealthy should only want to be friends with others who are wealthy and who really have nothing in common with the poor. Christians are not expected to openly be friends with nonbelievers because they might get tainted by bad behaviors. People sometimes also believe that the educated and uneducated cannot possibly have real dialogue about anything significant in life, and that two hearts cannot connect unless they have grown up together in the same neighborhood. In addition, we are sometimes warned not to befriend Middle Easterners who live in America because they might be terrorists. Of course, if such a thing were true, we would all have to bypass many urban cities with large populations of American-born ethnic Middle Easterners. I believe that there are times when we will have to break rank with other people's views and not always follow the popular vote so that we can follow our hearts and befriend and disciple someone others don't particularly like.

Throughout the years, I watched the cultural changes that occurred in my Chicago neighborhood and how it became increasingly more difficult to have separate play days and "territory" days in the alley as demographics changed and we became a more multicultural community. I also witnessed the huge discomfort that occurred as a result of people trying to avoid each other.

Many of the barriers we now experience in interacting with people who are perceived to be different from us have come from our own social constructions in a fear-based ideology that overlooks one important aspect: we have more in common as human beings than we really allow ourselves to believe. Friendship is not about connecting with people according to what they have accomplished or not accomplished or what they have or don't have.

Could the new model of diverse relationships consist of a wealthy man and a homeless man sitting together in the same coffee shop laughing, talking, sharing stories about pain and joys, and above all having a human relational experience that moves beyond tangible assets?

Pause Moment

- What are some ways we can pursue understanding different cultures, especially if we live or work in environments that are not diverse?

- How can we find more in common with people from diverse backgrounds?

- What Scriptures come to mind when you think of crossing barriers with others to bring unity and understanding?

show kindness
and give honor

Kindness is a VAST color that only
your heart knows how to paint.
RAKTIVIST

During spring 1981, one of my favorite persons at the time, Chicago mayor Jane Byrne, made the announcement that she and her husband were going to move into my old neighborhood: the Cabrini-Green housing projects. Cabrini-Green was one of the most infamous, notorious projects to live in. This was not because there were so many people with deviant behavior present there but rather because there were a few who made life miserable for the rest of us.

I could hardly believe it when the news reports announced that the mayor wanted to leave her home and come live with us in the projects as a resident and not a celebrity. I remember how excited all the residents were. It felt like such an honor that a person we really loved would be living with us to get a taste of our life for at least a year! I can't remember anyone saying that they wanted her to do something for them; it was just the thought and the symbolism of the idea. Thinking that we would be able to build community with her and introduce her to our world brought us joy.

Our projects had come to symbolize perpetual crime, urban blight, and the racial and classist divide within the city. While most of us who grew up in Cabrini-Green had no choice of whether we would stay there or not, Mayor Byrne did. Skeptical residents said it was a PR blitz, but it really didn't matter to most of us. It was a sign of hope for the community that not only a mayor but a white couple would actually live with residents in the projects and walk the streets, eat in the restaurants, and perhaps even curtail crime. Before Mayor Byrne even moved in, gang members held talks about calling truces.

The day for their move came, and they took up residence at Cabrini-Green on the first floor. Our excitement was short-lived though. No sooner was the announcement made than the floor they moved onto was totally transformed to accommodate them. The windows were replaced, elevators repaired, walkways swept, and flowers planted, and there was more visible police protection—around that building.

It was all nice. Unfortunately, though, the silent messages communicated to some of the residents were, "I can only live here if I transform the area to reflect what I deem is beautiful,"

"You are not worth getting elevators fixed or the building transformed unless I am part of it," and "The only building that is being transformed is the building that I will live in." We never heard anything negative spoken, but the perception that the mayor moving into our world would be a symbolic act of kindness and a gift to us fell flat; the move didn't feel like that to any of us.

I believe there were some good intentions behind the move, but they did not match the effect. In addition, when something happened that invoked fear in them three weeks after they moved in, they moved back out. I didn't know what had happened, and I still liked Mayor Byrne as a person, but the effect of what happened was damaging to the residents and community.

It's true that the Cabrini-Green projects were not the easiest place to live. One source gives this apt description:

During the worst years of Cabrini-Green's problems, vandalism increased substantially. Gang members and miscreants covered interior walls with graffiti and damaged doors, windows, and elevators. Rat and cockroach infestations were commonplace, rotting garbage stacked up in clogged trash chutes (it once piled up to the 15th floor), and basic utilities (water, electricity, etc.) often malfunctioned and were left unrepaired. On the exterior, boarded-up windows, burned-out areas of the façade, and pavement instead of green space—all in the name of economizing on maintenance—created an atmosphere of neglect and decay. The balconies were fenced in to prevent residents from emptying garbage cans into the yard, and from falling or being thrown to their deaths. This created the appearance of a large prison tier, or of animal cages.

But it was not the worst place to live. Behind all of the walls of the towering beige-and-white uniform brick projects were real men, women, and children. Not everyone who lived there was dysfunctional or in a gang. Many homes were intact with a father, a mother, and children. We also had honor students and college students in the projects. There were not many opportunities for people get to know each other, however.

But then some wonderful things started happening in our community. Interns from Moody Bible Institute had the courage to come and share the gospel of Christ with us and to have Bible studies on-site in some of the recreation rooms. Vibrant relationships rooted in the love of Christ were formed between the white interns and some of the residents.

Our community had full hearts for others and began fixing meals for our interns. We learned from talking to each other that, regardless of the side of town we lived on, we had some similar stories about life. Experiences of joy, pain, and sorrow connected some of us in the most unusual ways.

The example of the interns at the Cabrini-Green projects reminds me of how God sometimes gives us unique opportunities for building relationships where we never would have thought it was possible. These are opportunities to connect with someone at the heart level that God brings across our path or sends us to. A unique opportunity might come, for example, at the gym where we work out, when a person who speaks very little English continues to smile at us and then initiates a conversation, albeit in broken English.

However, we must also keep in mind that some lessons about culture and building community are learned best at a distance until there is a full readiness to engage fully with honor, respect, and dignity. The interns understood this.

Honoring by Seeing

The phrase "symbolic acts of kindness" means that by finding out what a person or culture deeply values, certain acts could be done to communicate a sense of value and dignity to a person. Doing something as simple as giving our full attention and full presence when we are with someone is a gift to them and an example of a symbolic act of kindness. It communicates to the person or persons that they matter.

I have a friend who shows me this type of kindness. He is always present when he is with me. What I mean is that he gives me the gift of his full focus and he listens. He has listened well enough to know foods that I like or don't like, he can look at the expression on my face and know when I'm having a challenging day, and he knows when he needs to talk and when he needs to listen. He has learned a lot about me just by observing and listening.

If we take the time to observe and learn from our friends, as my friend has for me, we won't have so many fears, and we won't have to walk on eggshells. It's true that listening well doesn't eliminate conflict; it takes wisdom to walk with someone in a manner that is pleasing and honoring to God without allowing the spirit of offense to be a driving force between us or compromising personal beliefs. No matter what kind of friendship we have with someone, offenses will at times come, and forgiveness has to be one of the foundations that holds the relationship together. But listening to get to know another person and being fully present with them can help minimize misunderstandings and conflict.

As I think about all of my close friends, I realize that I have a different relationship with each of them—and I should. I feel blessed to have both male and female friends and friends from so many diverse backgrounds. I don't think to say to people that I have a white friend or a Native American friend; I'll just say "my friend" because the color of a person's skin is not the basis of how I relate to them. I connect at the heart. However, I don't think I would be able to connect at the heart with any of my friends if I did not honor the beauty of who God has made them to be. Although it sounds good to say "I don't see color," and although the statement may come from a sincere heart, it's not an honoring comment to a person of color. If you don't see my color, you don't see me. It would almost be the same as receiving a beautiful bouquet of roses and asking what color they are, and then hearing the response, "I don't know because I don't see color."

God has created us in such a beautiful way that although we do see our skin color, it is a very minute thing in a genuine relationship and has no bearing on how we respond to each other. We learn about others and who they are through intentionally asking them questions.

Asking questions and listening to learn also keeps us from having *presumptuous understandings* about different cultures. The term means that a person believes that they know about an entire culture of people because they have had a brief encounter or experience with a person or situation that now makes them the expert. I can recount numerous times when I have heard comments such as, "I had a black friend just like you when I was growing up." I usually grin and respond that I am unique, and that while their friend and I perhaps have some similar traits, I am certain that the person they grew up with was not "just like me."

Presumptuous understandings can also take the form of assuming that we have a deeper relationship with someone different from us than we actually do because the relationship has never been proven or tested through time. Asking questions that communicate we see someone else as an individual and want to get to know them as such—as a unique human created in God's image—honors them and helps build a foundation for authentic relationship.

Kindness in a Remote Desert

My first trip to Africa in 2000 was to the country of Kenya. I was excited to finally travel to a place that had been on my heart for over a decade.

I didn't know what to expect in Nairobi, but I felt that I was going to have an incredible short-term missions trip back in the home of my African roots! I knew that I would automatically connect with the motherland just because. But I had also spent a lot of time with black people who had traveled to Kenya, and when they returned to the United States most would say that their lives had been changed by the kindness of the people there.

A team of us traveled from the United States to Kenya with the purpose of talking about economic development and leadership, and speaking at high schools throughout Nairobi. When we arrived, we got to experience the foods of the land right away, as our first team meal was at a restaurant where I was treated to Kenyan food and warm soda. And I found an excitement for the gospel that I had not known in a while. It was also interesting to find that certain areas of the city have a Western influence. Some of the young people asked me if I could teach them how to do hip-hop dancing.

But even though I met incredibly wonderful people in Nairobi, I didn't feel an automatic connection and quickly realized that the color of my skin alone would not connect me to this country that has such a vibrant cultural history—one that is not tied to America.

I tried to immediately let people know that I had global etiquette by making surface remarks, such as "I know that the only language in the country is Swahili," to which came the response, "Not really. We have over sixty-two languages." I also made a lot of comments that were rooted in me trying way too hard to let my African brothers and sisters know that I was one of them. I didn't need to do all of that, however, and the comments only served to make me come across as an arrogant American.

But then I had a human experience that connected me on a deep level, beyond the surface. During my first week in Kenya, I was given the privilege of speaking about leadership to a group of students at a high school. I had prayed that God would give me words of encouragement for the young people about their identity and about how they have a purpose beyond what they could see.

The day I delivered my talk was beautiful, and the young people were brought outside to sit on the grass around me. They were attentive and very receptive. During the middle of my talk, I slapped my right leg because it felt like I had been bitten by an insect. I didn't think much about it until the following evening, when my right leg became numb and black and was oozing with sores. The pain became so intense that I was taken to a clinic on the outskirts of Nairobi. The nurses informed me that I had been bitten by a poisonous insect. When the local clinic could not help me because of having limited medications, my hosts and a few team members hauled me in a medical van on a rugged road to a more prominent clinic in the city. It was a two-hour journey.

Because I had started out with arrogance and pride when I arrived in Kenya, I didn't think anyone would really care about how I felt now, so I wanted to be strong. But being in pain brought me face-to-face with my helplessness and with the possibility of losing a leg in a country that I had only been in for a week. I cried out, and at some point one of the women took her fist and began pounding my leg nonstop. Others took turns as well. To my surprise, the only relief from pain that I had in those two hours in a hot van over an unpaved road was having people pound on my leg. Their nonstop action for such a long time deeply touched my heart.

Everyone in the van also comforted me by singing to me, telling jokes, and simply being kind. As I think about the concept of Ubuntu—*I am because we are*—I can see the "we are" on that journey to the clinic. It was a humble reminder to me that in my suffering I connected with a kind nation of people who only wanted to see me as a human being, not as an American coming to their country insisting that I was a gift to them. It was the other way around.

Pause Moment

- How do you honor those from different cultures? Is it appropriate to ask a person from a different culture what honor looks like to them and then proceed to demonstrate it (that is, a symbolic act of kindness)?

- In Acts 27 the apostle Paul and others were shipwrecked on the island of Malta. In Acts 28:1-2, once the shipwrecked people were safely onshore, the islanders showed them "unusual kindness." What does it mean to show someone extraordinary kindness?

revisit assumptions and embrace cultural learning

What we need to do is learn to respect and embrace our differences until our differences don't make a difference in how we are treated.

YOLANDA KING

During November 2012, I embarked on a spiritual journey and quest to gain greater clarity about God's purposes for my life. I had gotten weary of my duties as a professor and my responsibilities as an associate minister at my church, especially the myriad of meetings. And I was overwhelmed by life. I loved everything I was doing but felt I needed time to breathe, pray, reevaluate my life, and gain fresh insights about this book.

I packed my bags, put my items in storage, took a leave of absence from responsibilities in Colorado, and traveled back to my home state of Illinois, to a small motel on the border of Illinois and Indiana. I had booked a long-term reservation on a travel site, and although I didn't have a chance to really choose where I was going to stay, it was a name-brand motel and the price that I bid on was great!

However, when I arrived, I was totally disappointed with the upkeep of the motel. The floor was so dirty that I put one of my bed sheets on the floor to walk on. I also noticed that some of the residents at the hotel looked very ragged and worn down from life. And though I thought all of the front desk staff were warm and friendly, I wondered why people would come into the lobby late at night and get free food. In assessing the situation, I wore very big "assumption glasses"— the glasses I use when I don't know the truth about a situation and instead assume that I know and make my decisions based on my assumptions.

I assumed, for example, that the reason the motel was so cheap when I bid online was because it was really a drug motel. I also assumed that the motel had intentionally hired cleaning staff who didn't speak English because it was easier to hide the drug activities from them.

I decided to put my "Please do not disturb" sign on my door and leave it there to let the cleaning staff know that I would control when they came into my room to clean. Then I locked myself in the room and didn't leave except to eat and get fresh air.

After being there a week, though, something strange happened. I started feeling lonely. What I thought was going to be a wonderful month away turned out to not be so fun after all. I found myself daily going to sit in the lobby to talk with people. And although I still didn't like the motel, I felt my heart connecting with the mom and dad who came down to the lobby every day with their infant, and with the crippled man who stood at the front desk, just wanting to talk.

I was still making assumptions though. For example, I noticed the cleaning staff staring at me each time I left my hotel room, so I assumed they were saying something bad about me. I would peek out of my room at them—the motel did not have an inside corridor—and watch them daily pulling heavy bins of laundry and supplies to clean the rooms. My heart was drawn to one lady especially who worked in the cold without a coat. I kept looking at my coat—my favorite coat—and wondered what she would think if I offered it to her.

When I had first heard the housekeeping staff speak I thought they were Hispanic, but very quickly I recognized that they were Filipino and were speaking their native language, Tagalog. In a previous role of mine at an international missions organization I was privileged to travel around the world and throughout America, connecting with different cultures in very unique places. One of the places I found new friends was in an Asian community in San Francisco with a group of Filipina and Chinese women.

After my second week at the motel, I finally got up the courage to go speak to the cleaning staff. I wanted to at least say hello and offer a smile. I also thought I could let them know that I know who the Filipino Puerto Rican musician Gary Valenciano (or Gary V., as he's usually called) is and that I actually have one of his CDs, in hopes that maybe he could be a common point of reference and helpful conversation starter. In addition, given that I had constructed a flawed mental explanation that their staring at me was based on their immediate dislike of me, I was thinking that they would probably quit talking about me if I said hi.

I approached them and began to speak very slowly. "Hellooo, my name is MelindaJoy." I carefully articulated my words on the outside chance that they could *possibly* understand English. The women started laughing, and one of them politely said back to me slowly in perfect English, "Hellooo, we speak English." It was a moment that we laughed about throughout the rest of my time at the motel and again another lesson for me in assuming I know about people.

I learned that they had been wanting to connect with me from the time I arrived, but since I had kept my "Do not disturb" sign on my door, they thought I didn't want to be disturbed. No, we did not become the best of friends, but my motel room became the room of fellowship and fun, as four of the women would always stop by after they were done with work. I even found that they were Christians. When I became ill for two days, one of the women knocked at my door offering a huge bowl of soup that the cleaning staff bought for me. I thanked her and cried in humility after I shut the door. To think that people who had just met me would sacrifice their meager finances to buy soup for me was incredible.

I found out that, when I had first checked in, the front desk staff had told the cleaning staff that I was probably a pretty wealthy person because I had paid to stay so many nights and also because I had signed my name as "Dr." on the receipt. This made me cry again as I thought back on how snooty I had been when I arrived because I didn't like the place and how God had given me a second chance to connect with the most wonderful people I had ever known. I also eventually found out before I left that although the place was a bona fide motel, a section of it was rented out by the city to house the homeless. This explained to me the reason why some of the people there looked so destitute and homeless— it's because they were.

I cried yet again when my last night at the motel came and all of my new friends—even the mom and dad with their infant son—met me in the lobby to give me notes and cards they had written for me. I had made friends with an elderly black man who was well into his eighties and had shared his stories with me of walking through the civil rights movement with Dr. Martin Luther King Jr., with my Filipina sisters, with the front desk staff who were Indian, and with the young white couple and their son who had lost their apartment because of a job loss.

Okay. *Really, God? Did I need to travel all the way to Crestwood, Illinois, for a month to find that my purpose is to express your heart for others?* Yes. At the motel I heard the term in my spirit—*Ubuntu.* My coat ended up being one way I experienced that. I offered my coat to the woman who did not have one as I left the motel and headed on a bus to my next stop in Gary, Indiana. But no more than a week later a lady asked me if she could give me her coat because she had so many. I also thought about my life of homelessness and feeling displaced, which prepared me for my experience at the motel and sharing life experiences that did not have color, race, or economic status attached to them. They had the grace of God's goodness woven throughout.

I really do believe God has moments of holy laughter as he looks at us. We create so many fears about relating to others when he, of course, knows it is all part of a bigger plan for his purposes to be achieved through us and his love for all people to be put on display as we remember that each person is created in his image. We must revisit our assumptions.

Becoming Learners

One of the greatest gifts we can give to people from other cultures is cultivating and embracing the heart of a learner. We don't have to feel that we know everything; it's good to walk in humility and gratefulness with those we call friends, who are really God's gifts to us.

Two of my friends, Josay and Caris, are Norwegian immigrants. They have traveled all over the world making disciples and equipping others in their spiritual walk. Josay and Caris shared their story with me about being learners in a new culture in Zambia.

When they met Tufa, a graduate of the University of Zambia, Josay said, "Tufa, it is likely that I will cause offense in some way as a newcomer to Zambia. What could help me minimize offense?"

Tufa said, "Are you sure you want me to be that honest?" Josay assured him he did.

Tufa responded, "When I come to your home and you open the door, don't say, 'Hi, Tufa, what can I do for you?' For us that is very rude. Invite me in, offer me something to drink, ask about my family. Once we have covered all these things, then I will tell you why I have come."

Learning to ask about family, in particular, is very important in Africa, perhaps because of their "I am because we are" perspective. Africans carry their families close to their hearts. When you show interest in the extended family, you say you care about them. I do this with Americans as well, since caring for our friends' families, not just the individual, is a holistic thing to do and says I really care about what they are going through. Perhaps it also expresses the truth that we are shaped by our families, and how our family is doing says something about how we are as well.

Josay and Caris explained to me that Tufa's lesson helped them a lot about taking time for relationships. One day they even heard their toddler at the door, saying "Come in, come in. Want a drink?"

Josay recounted,

I learned similar lessons during a trip in Cameroon. We traveled over high mountain roads, only partly paved, with our driver using the emergency brake to slow us down on the hills. Then we arrived in pouring rain during a power outage, not knowing who would pick us up. By a miracle, someone knew someone else who informed the local host that we had arrived, and we were taken to a guest house, cold, damp, and hungry. Slowly, things were prepared for us.

The next day we spoke at a combined church conference where it was extremely hot. Afterward, we were asked if we would join the pastors for lunch. It was tempting to say, in our fatigue, "No thanks, we would rather go back and rest," especially knowing that most of the pastors did not speak English. But we responded, "Yes, we would love to," and enjoyed a very typical meal of fufu and njama, which we came to love. Later the host pastor said, "That was so good that you did not refuse hospitality. Otherwise, you would have had no credibility with us."

Accepting hospitality and expressing appreciation are important in all cultures. Showing honor to guests, as the host pastors had done for me and my team in Kenya, is also taken very seriously in many cultures. The food in Africa, by American standards, might appear simple. But it was always very carefully prepared, showing care for hygiene issues. And it was never carelessly thrown down; rather, it was carefully placed, showing real respect for guests. Another part of the African meal tradition that shows honor is offering a basin of warm water, soap, and a towel for washing our hands before the food is served. The host or a family member will often kneel while you are seated to serve you in this way, going from one guest to another, and from those who are older and more respected to those who are younger.

Hospitality always included food for Josay and Caris. Josay tells of going to meet his Kenyan boss's family. They took two buses and two matatus (small pickup trucks with benches in the back) and then walked several miles to the family home in the hills. Even though they were not able to stay long and they were far from convenience stores, the mother (one of three wives) carefully prepared a boiled egg and a cup of tea as a snack for them. It was what she had. Africans will always share what they have, even if it is not fancy food. If you are there, you are invited and expected to join in.

When I traveled to Addis Ababa on a missions trip, I learned that Ethiopian coffee ceremonies are a wonderful way to experience hospitality. The coffee beans are brought home green from the market. When the guests arrive, the host begins roasting the beans in a pan over a charcoal fire while the visitors watch. The dirt or cement floor has been covered with long, fresh grass. Once the beans are roasted, making the home smell wonderful, they are ground in a hand grinder, allowing more time for conversation. Finally, the water is heated over the same charcoal fire and poured over the coffee in a special pot. When fully brewed, the coffee is served to the guests in handleless cups, with butter and salt added for flavor. Typically a cob of corn is offered on the side as a snack. The purpose of the coffee ceremony is to savor the time, as well as the coffee. It is not a quick cup, but it is a celebration of relationship, a time for communing, not to be hurried.

When we are fearful of different people groups, we often become paralyzed and don't know how to be intentional in befriending someone. By accepting offers of hospitality and expressing appropriate appreciation for the ways we've been served by others, genuine relationships can begin to develop.

Pause Moment

- Can you think of a time when you have communicated "do not disturb" as it pertains to relationships? If so, why do you think you did that?

- Have you ever given thought to the fact that your interaction with someone from a different class might be the one encounter a person needs to realize they are a person of worth?

- Describe a situation in which you felt honored by someone. What did they do that made you feel that way?

- Think of someone you've been wanting to honor. What is one step you can take to begin to do that?

conclusion and next steps

*Most of my important lessons about life
have come from recognizing how others
from a different culture view things.*

EDGAR H. SCHEIN

If you have read this far through the book or even skipped to the end, I want to leave you with hope, faith, and optimism. You *can* connect with people from diverse backgrounds and shatter the barriers of race, gender, class, and any other thing that divides us. And many of you are already cultural champions. You are learning about diverse people groups, becoming bicultural, and moving from surface-only relationships to authentic ones in your workplace, home, school, and neighborhoods.

I encourage you to take small steps, if necessary, toward initiating relationships with people of different cultures.

Many times God transforms us through unseen work in our hearts. Other times the Lord unexpectedly knits together different people's lives, which becomes the catalyst for change.

We see the outer picture of beauty in relationships with God and others that are rooted in honesty, integrity, and his design for our lives. Because God continually wants to reveal himself to us in order for us to truly know him, he allows us to see his heart more clearly through our relationships and how we treat each other.

If you are used to befriending people who think like you, act like you, or even look like you, step out in faith and don't let fear paralyze you. I have friends from every walk of life, every race, and every kind of lifestyle. One of my best friends is a man who has been homeless for over a year. We simply connect as human beings and talk about life. I also have friends who aren't religious and don't have the hope of Jesus, but they are my friends who need to hear the message of hope. If someone feels destitute, they don't care what your race is—they just want hope. Ultimately, I want my life to encourage every person and affirm their value, worth, and dignity as a fellow human being. And I want to obey Jesus' command to go and make disciples.

Facing Fear with Our Head, Heart, or Gut

I remember watching *The Wizard of Oz* movie at least twenty times as a child and being particularly fascinated with one scene. It is the scene that depicts the main characters— Dorothy, the Tin Man, the Scarecrow, and the Cowardly Lion— trembling and scared out of their wits as they walk down a corridor to approach the Wizard of Oz, who has been harassing them. The pivotal point for me in the movie comes when the little dog, Toto, pulls the curtain away from the domain of the wizard only to reveal that the culprit is a mere four feet tall and becomes more fearful than any of the main characters when he is discovered as being powerless.

This movie is a somewhat humorous yet helpful picture of the different ways we can respond to fear: with our *head*, *heart*, or *gut*. When we are faced with an opportunity to confront the very thing we have feared, we sometimes forge ahead with our *head*—specifically, with head knowledge, symbolized by the Scarecrow, who believes that if he receives a brain he will be able think his way through fear and will be all right. The *heart* is symbolized by the Tin Man, who believes that he has to feel his way to courage. My favorite character was actually the Cowardly Lion, who is so steeped in fear that he figuratively jumps out of his skin when his own tail hits him and frightens him. He has to press through overwhelming fear and have the *guts* to continue on his journey, which means courage is only necessary when we need to conquer fear. We can't always think or feel our way through building cross-cultural relationships—or any relationship for that matter. And it especially takes courage to forge ahead with a relationship in which we've been hurt or misunderstood, or that feels like too much work. Here are a few suggestions and reflection questions for moving through our fears.

Your "gut" moment. Can you pause and think about the person or people you've wanted to befriend or build a relationship with but have been paralyzed with fear that you will be rejected or will trip over your own tail in the process? Is there someone of a different culture or lifestyle from yours? What can you do to push past your comfort zone to be intentional in pursuing the relationship?

Your "head" moment. Have you been trying to think your way out of befriending someone who makes you feel uncomfortable because you fear what others will think and the rules of society keep ringing in your head? If so, what do you believe your response should be to the Lord's prompting to be courageous and model a new pattern (Romans 12:2)?

Your "heart" moment. Can you recall connecting with someone and immediately feeling a heart connection that you knew had been prompted by the Holy Spirit? This is a reminder that when we are open to receiving the gift of friendship, it doesn't take long to connect with someone from a diverse background.

We Are Alike and Unique

I love the statement "In certain respects, every person behaves like all others: in other respects, like some others . . . and in some cases, like no others." We are "like all others" speaks to me about our humanity. We can travel throughout the world and find people wrestling with pain and suffering or enjoying the birth of a baby. When I see the tragedy of a plane crash in another part of the world and the images on television of people weeping and grieving over their loss, my heart is moved. And as I have traveled to the slums of Ethiopia, served in AIDS clinics, and witnessed extreme poverty firsthand, my heart has connected with people beyond words. Similarly, I have experienced universal joy and fun dancing to Latin music at a Vietnamese university with people from Singapore, Vietnam, Australia, and other countries. Building relationships is about learning how to do life with people who have similar interests and sharing stories along the way.

We are "like some others" reflects the vital component of our learned culture and why there are some people who we will automatically gravitate to because of shared cultural behaviors. I admittedly find intentional ways to stay connected to my black culture because there are some things that another black person may understand that a nonblack person might not. For example, there are black songs and musical artists I like and that I want someone else to know as well. Or I might want to talk with someone who will understand why the customs of eating banana pudding, black-eyed peas, fried chicken, and cornbread on New Year's Day is important to me. I'm not saying these things are necessarily healthy by a medical standard; they're just important to who I am and where I have been in life, and were a real part of shaping me in what I like versus don't like. Similarly, some friends understand me and I know will not reprimand me when I say honestly that, while I do love organic food and healthy food, being poor is a journey, and when you are limited in finances, you look up to heaven and thank God even for food from a dollar store. I want to sometimes merely rest and not have to explain my hair or my dialect or be the representative for all actions in the black community.

We are "like no others" helps us embrace the important fact that we are wonderfully and fearfully formed by the hands of God. If no snowflake is the same, surely we can celebrate even more our individual uniqueness. This phrase also reflects the fact that there are times when we may feel very different from anyone else present in a particular place or situation we find ourselves. For me, this happens when the integrity of my spiritual culture and what I believe as a Christian are being violated; in those instances I keep my values and beliefs close to my heart. As both Christians who are called to be different from the world—people of love and true disciples of Jesus—and as ones made uniquely and purposefully by God, we have to be comfortable with the spiritual transformation that takes place as Jesus continues to shape and fashion us each as individuals.

I decided to complete my book at one of my favorite local donut shops. I thought it would be a perfectly fun place to write, eat a donut, of course, and meet people. I was not disappointed, and I truly believe that Jesus had such a wonderful story for me to share as part of the conclusion of this book.

The donut shop is a favorite hangout for both young and old. I had been seated for about five minutes when a lady I had never met came to my table and asked me if I wanted some pizza. Oddly enough, I said yes, and we embarked on a conversation in which we shared similar stories of losing our mothers over the past few months and our journeys through the loss.

When she left, two young women came and stood in front of me with a box of donuts and jokingly said to me, "Choose a row and a donut and it's yours!" Deciding to play along with them, I chose my second donut within the past half hour and laughed as they told me a bit of their stories.

Thinking that my book's final story was complete, I spent three hours at a table where people came by and wanted to talk. I wanted to share that I didn't have time to talk because I was writing a book on how to build relationships. But I thought that would baffle everyone who was trying to make some type of connection with me.

I had a good time hanging out with people who wanted donuts and conversations. After three hours of being in the shop—and two cups of free coffee, two slices of pizza, and three donuts—I decided my mission was accomplished. I was *full*, literally and figuratively.

Did I finish my book? No. But my time at the donut shop was a reminder to me that so many people are waiting for an invitation to connect with someone, even if it's over a cup of coffee. The gift of our presence can be the best connection a person has for the day.

Moving Forward in Diverse Friendships

I want to leave you with some next steps as you intentionally pursue diverse cultural relationships.

- Ask God to give you the wisdom you need to reach diverse people.

- Study and model the life of Jesus and his relational style with others for the sake of the gospel.

- Be intentional about connecting with diverse people, and forge beyond discomforts for the benefit and beauty of the friendship.

- Develop a go-to versus a come-to attitude about diverse experiences. Don't wait for people to come to you; go to them.

- Desire to become a cultural champion in your community, place of worship, and everyday living.

- Remember that our walk as followers of Christ will draw others to us.

- Be willing to stand courageously against any type of racial injustice directed toward your friends and close acquaintances.

- Develop listening skills as you connect with different cultures, not just for the sake of listening but in order to demonstrate the value, worth, and dignity of people from different backgrounds.

- Suspend judgments about people, and don't allow stereotypes of different people groups to be reinforced. Develop skills to connect in relevant and empathetic ways with people.

- Walk in humility as a learner, and be willing to also teach others about your culture.

- Don't allow yourself to be color blind. Enjoy the beauty that each person brings into a relationship.

- Remember that people are more alike than they are different.

- Move out of your comfort zone and stay out of it. Don't let anxiety, misinformation, or biases prevent you from reaching someone God has been putting on your heart.

- Take the initiative to love and befriend people. (Yes, you!)

- Be careful about letting past negative attempts and experiences with someone from another culture mark or affect your present experiences. Don't feel that you have to walk on eggshells with people from different cultures. Allow mistakes to be a catalyst for learning new things about others.

- Ask Jesus to show you things you may be unconsciously doing that communicate dishonor to others who are different from you.

- Think about the times when you have felt unwanted in an environment. Then look at patterns, acts of rejection, or apathy that you have held or practiced toward other cultures.

- Embrace an Ubuntu philosophy of compassion, empathy, and dignity, and not just with the people you like.
- Learn to engage by taking seriously the need to learn.

Ubuntu "is the essence of being human. It speaks of the fact that my humanity is caught up and is inextricably bound up in yours. I am human because I belong. It speaks about wholeness, it speaks about compassion. . . .

"[People with Ubuntu] know that they are diminished when others are humiliated, diminished when others are oppressed, diminished when others are treated as if they were less than who they are." Ubuntu represent the value, worth, and dignity of every human being.

May Jesus go with you as you build relationships and continually learn and embrace the beauty of diverse friendships.

acknowledgments

I am beyond grateful to the many persons I have journeyed with and become friends with from around the world who have been instrumental in the completion of this book. I will always have a heart and love for Vietnam and the years of teaching, speaking, dancing, and having fun with the professors and students at Hanoi University. Thank you both Brian and Ginny Teel of REI (Resource Exchange International) for inviting me to try a new leadership experience in Vietnam that would forever change my life.

I love my cultural learning journeys and friends in Kenya, Ethiopia, and Santo Domingo who have left fingerprints of love in my heart.

To my beloved sister, Vicki Carter, you are one of the most loving persons that I know. As I have watched your life, you have taught me much about the beauty of seeing people beyond the surface.

My thanks are extended to Pastor Promise Lee of Relevant Word Ministries for the encouragement to think beyond what I could presently see to what I felt God wanted me to do. I love the numerous conversations we've had over the years about social justice and culture. Your experience and wisdom with diverse groups of people has taught me a lot about how to introduce Christ into society and culture in meaningful ways.

Mary Lancaster, you are beyond a friend to me and have walked with me through so many difficult situations in my life, including my "desert experience" of truly learning about God through your love for me. You have cared for me through homelessness, lack, and despair, and have been the heart and hands of Jesus to me.

To Tom and Carol McLennan, my friends for life, your love and prayers for me and this book have meant much.

While I can't list every name of fellow travelers along the journey of life who mean so much to me, I will list your name and give you virtual big hugs: Teri Greiner, June Jones, Alfreda Jones, Jadonna Brewton, Tina Marsh, Laura Calhoun, Kalena Gibbs, and my Near Frontiers family.

Lastly, I am beyond grateful to my friend and mentor, Calvin Johnson. Thank you for being the catalyst of encouragement for me through every aspect of this journey to craft this message. I am grateful for all of our prayer times surrounding this book and your encouragement for me to keep my eyes focused on Jesus through this process. You are a steady model of love, compassion, and truth, and are the heart of the Father to all people, which encourages me to live the message that I write about.

notes

3   Ubuntu—*how can one of us:* Christine Miller, "UBUNTU, How Can One of Us Be Happy If All the Other Ones Are Sad?" LoveWorks, accessed February 18, 2020, www.loveworks.co/2013/04/24/ubuntu-how-can-one-of-us -be-happy-if-all-the-other-ones-are-sad.

4   *It is the essence:* "Understanding the Essence of Ubuntu—The African Philosophy," Historyplex, accessed February 18, 2020, https://historyplex .com/ubuntu-african-philosophy.

31   *In the 1940s, two black psychologists:* "The Significance of 'the Doll Test,'" NAACP Legal Defense and Education Fund, accessed February 20, 2020, www.naacpldf.org/ldf-celebrates-60th-anniversary-brown-v-board-edu cation/significance-doll-test.

     According to Chief Justice Earl Warren: "Brown v. Board of Education: The First Step in the Desegregation of America's School," History, updated August 31, 2018, www.history.com/news/brown-v-board-of-education-the -first-step-in-the-desegregation-of-americas-schools.

33   *a brightly colored dashiki:* A dashiki is a colorful, loose garment of West Africa worn by women and men. It is called *kitenge* in East Africa and has been a dominant garment in Tanzania and later in Kenya.

35   *We need to give each other:* Max De Pree, "Max De Pree Quotes," BrainyQuote, accessed February 18, 2020, www.brainyquote.com/quotes /max_de_pree_125756.

79   *During the worst years*: "Cabrini-Green Homes," Wikipedia, accessed January 8, 2020, https://en.wikipedia.org/wiki/Cabrini-Green_Homes.

102 *every person behaves like all others:* Felicity Menzies, "Understanding One Another: How You Are Like All Others, Like Some Others, and Like No Others," Include-Power.com, accessed February 20, 2020, https://culture plusconsulting.com/2016/02/16/understanding-one-another-how-you-are -like-all-others-like-some-others-and-like-no-others.

108 *the essence of being human:* "Understanding the Essence of Ubuntu—The African Philosophy," Historyplex, accessed February 18, 2020, https://history plex.com/ubuntu-african-philosophy.

recommended resources

Michelle Alexander, *The New Jim Crow: Mass Incarceration in the Age of Color-blindness*

David A. Anderson, *Gracism: The Art of Inclusion*

Richard Dahlstrom, *The Colors of Hope: Becoming People of Mercy, Justice, and Love*

Duane Elmer, *Cross-Cultural Servanthood: Serving the World in Christlike Humility*

Michael O. Emerson and Christian Smith, *Divided by Faith: Evangelical Religion and the Problem of Race in America*

Gary Haugen, *Good News About Injustice: A Witness of Courage in a Hurting World*

Bethany Hanke Hoang and Kristen Deede Johnson, *The Justice Calling: Where Passion Meets Perseverance*

Willie Jennings, *The Christian Imagination: Theology and the Origins of Race*

Tim Keller, *Generous Justice: How God's Grace Makes Us Just*

Patty Lane, *A Beginner's Guide to Crossing Cultures: Making Friends in a Multi-cultural World*

Bryan Loritts, ed., *Letters to a Birmingham Jail: A Response to the Words and Dreams of Dr. Martin Luther King, Jr.*

Joel W. Martin and Mark A. Nicholas, eds., *Native Americans, Christianity, and the Reshaping of the American Religious Landscape*

Brenda Salter McNeil and Rick Richardson, *The Heart of Racial Justice: How Soul Change Leads to Social Change*

John Perkins, *One Blood: Parting Words to the Church on Race and Love*

John Perkins, *With Justice for All: A Strategy for Community Development*

Robert J. Priest and Alvaro L. Nieves, eds., *This Side of Heaven: Race, Ethnicity, and Christian Faith*

Soong-Chan Rah, *Many Colors: Cultural Intelligence for a Changing Church*

Soong-Chan Rah, *Prophetic Lament: A Call for Justice in Troubled Times*

Doug Serven, ed., *Heal Us, Emmanuel: A Call for Racial Reconciliation, Representation, and Unity in the Church*

Clarence Shuler, *Winning the Race to Unity: Is Racial Reconciliation Really Working?*

Bryan Stevenson, *Just Mercy: A Story of Justice and Redemption*

Ken Wytsma, *Pursuing Justice: The Call to Live and Die for Bigger Things*